Jean Baudrillard: Live Theory

Paul Hegarty

continuum
LONDON • NEW YORK

CONTINUUM
The Tower Building
11 York Road
London SE1 7NX

15 East 26th Street
New York
NY 10010

British Library Cataloguing-in-Publication Data
A catalogue record for this book is available from the British Library.

ISBN: HB: 0–8264–6282–0
         PB: 0–8264–6283–9

Library of Congress Cataloging-in-Publication Data
Hegarty, Paul, 1954–
   Jean Baudrillard : live theory / Paul Hegarty.
      p.   cm.
   Includes bibliographical references and index.
   ISBN 0–8264–6282–0 – ISBN 0–8264–6283–9 (pbk.)
   1. Baudrillard, Jean. 2. Philosophers–France.   I. Title.
   B2430.B33974H44 2004
   194–dc22   2003068809

Typeset by Servis Filmsetting Ltd, Manchester.
Printed and bound in Great Britain by MPG Books Ltd, Bodmin, Cornwall

Contents

Acknowledgements

Many people have contributed to the existence of this book, consciously or otherwise. I wish to thank the following in particular: Graham Allen, Jackie Clarke, Pat Crowley, Mike Gane, Malcolm Garrard, Gary Genosko, Martin Halliwell, Colin Harrison, Arthur and Marilouise Kroker, Caitríona Leahy, Dave Murray, Joanne O'Brien, Tony O'Connor, Brian O'Shaughnessy, Keith Reader, Judith Still, Stephen Walker, Alex Walsh and John Younge.

Special thanks to Tristan Palmer and Hywel Evans at Continuum.

For his acute observations and daemonic hyphen-cutting, thanks again to Graham Allen.

Thanks, finally, to Jean Baudrillard for his time, generosity and interest.

Note on References

In the main body of the text, all texts are referred to by their title, or by a shortened title when appropriate. Further details are to be found in the Bibliography. All texts by Baudrillard are referred to by their English title. The page number in the English version comes first, and every reference is accompanied by the page reference in the French original. Where there is an existing translation, it is referred to. If not, the translations are my own. The interview (Chapter 6) was conducted in French and translated by me.

Introduction

Jean Baudrillard has been a global theoretical presence for many years now, emerging in the late 1960s, alongside writers such as Michel Foucault, Jean-François Lyotard, Jacques Derrida and Gilles Deleuze. His writings address virtually all phenomena of the contemporary world: war, celebrity, information and communication technology, the end of Marxism, reality TV, the fate of history, graffiti, 9/11, photography, architecture, cloning . . . This range, and contemporary focus, are what gives his work its unique position among that influential generation of French thinkers, and have meant interest in his work spreads far beyond the academic world. His key ideas are symbolic exchange and simulation, and from simulation he derives his thought on the virtual, and on the contemporary body. The various forms of simulation are essential to an understanding of media and technology today, and how these have been theorized.

It is not just the content that sets Baudrillard apart, the style of his writings is also crucial here. The writers mentioned above all have their particular methods, and some sort of lineage from Nietzsche, but Baudrillard, except in his earlier writings, is the most intransigent of the lot, the one always beyond the pale, as nothing is to be accepted, no critique or method recommended, no academic convention followed. Since the 1980s, his texts have become increasingly aphoristic, speculative, and often free of argument as such. Instead there is a wall of assertions, claims, twists of logic, fictions, spews of metaphors losing their representative value, as they become something both more and less.

Baudrillard writes on, and sometimes the world catches up. At many points, the world resists, with readers in search of a politically critical perspective being disappointed, even enraged by Baudrillard. The English-speaking world provides a huge audience for Baudrillard's books, but also the most vociferous critique. The 1980s saw a huge number of critiques or even analyses of something called postmodernism. Whether this phenomenon was to be thought of as good or evil, Baudrillard would always be found at the extreme (something he would be happy with), either as the moment it 'all went too far' or as the exemplary version of why postmodernism and/or French thought in general was not to be trusted.[1] This body of writing, often semi-literate and badly researched, has received plenty of attention, but now that they have gone quiet on Baudrillard (other than a cameo in Alan Sokal and Jean Bricmont's risible *Intellectual Impostures*), and postmodernism is losing whatever capacities it had, we need not waste too much time over it here. The essential problem, for those critical of Baudrillard, lay in his removal, through analyses of the 'real world', of reality. His theory of simulation, which underpins all his thought of the past thirty years, was seen as politically apathetic. The irony, if that's what it is, is that the world increasingly looks like Baudrillard's idea of it, and his writings on politics, which have, for example, concentrated on the mediatization of 'democratic' politics, the decline of socialism even as the Left starts winning elections across Europe, the growth of terrorism, and the shift from classes to masses, are, almost certainly despite his wishes, political, even if not ideologically partisan.

Baudrillard is a commentator who has established a world system that is both porous and hermetic. He is able to deal with an enormous range of subjects, but like the black holes he often mentions as metaphors of the social, his system sucks those phenomena in, and closes them off.[2] Baudrillard's views, whether the reader believes them to be right or wrong, are very difficult to put to use, or to apply directly. Of course, it is possible to see this as their strength (as a form of Bataillean sovereignty, for example), and that this means his texts become theoretical objects, rather than being pieces for someone else's puzzle. It also means that even if the texts might resist critical interpretation, and even encourage critical misinterpretations, they provide platforms to build on. The often fragmentary nature of Baudrillard's writing also means that the reader can choose to focus on certain aspects or moments. The reader also has to be ready to be constantly challenged, whether at the 'macro' level, where reality dissipates, but returns as the hyperreal, the more real than real, or at individual moments where Baudrillard goes against conclusions we have too swiftly drawn on the basis of that general theory. The readership has changed over time, in any case, and has different expectations. Whereas the early books emerged into a world dominated by leftist critical writing, much of it still surprisingly dogmatic, and developed what could be described as a post-Marxist position on culture, this was gradually replaced, and finally disposed of by the mid-1970s. Readers of the early critical literature on Baudrillard, such as Douglas Kellner's *Jean Baudrillard*, Kellner and Best's *Postmodern Theory*, and even Mike Gane's *Baudrillard's Bestiary* might be bemused by the attention paid to the turn from Marxism, but 1970s France was still a place where leftist thought might have been rejuvenated, after the revolt of May 1968, the Maoist terrorism of the early 1970s and the Parti Communiste's slow crawl to electoral acceptability, while, later on, English-speaking culture was developing cultural studies as a critical discipline. The reception of Baudrillard was much more positive in North America, and in Canada, in particular, where Baudrillard was the key figure in a 'postmodern scene' comprising, at its core, Arthur and Marilouise Kroker, David Cook, Charles Levin, and existing presently in the form of the web journal *ctheory*. This support, along with Baudrillard's popularity outside academia, increased the ire of British critics. There is no doubt that whether read positively or negatively, Baudrillard is often misread or under-read. Nowhere is this more the case than in his relation to postmodernity and postmodernism, which is regularly asserted, even though the weight of evidence is against it.

The postmodern

Mike Gane has always sought to disassociate Baudrillard from postmodernism, and has recently argued that Baudrillard 'is drawn to and repulsed by the development of postmodern theory' (*Jean Baudrillard: In Radical Uncertainty*, p. 22). Baudrillard himself rejects the idea that his own work is postmodern, and reserves his use of the word for descriptions of fairly inane cultural practices. Why, then, is he almost universally held to be the leader of post-modernism? The answer lies in superficiality: first, in the rise of the superficial, the apparent, in recent history; second, Baudrillard's interest in simulation, the virtual and the fractal suggests he is somehow an apologist for this condition; third, superficial readings have highlighted some ideas in isolation, and have created a pre-sumption that what he writes, because it is free of recognizable ideological critique, is uncritical of what it sees.

When Baudrillard writes that the screen has replaced the scene (*The Ecstasy of Communication*, p. 12; 12), it seems close to Frederic Jameson's notion of 'the loss of affect', or to those who bemoan some lost sociality, but Baudrillard is, above all, disinterested. From his point of view, so-called postmodern theory has not completed its own logic if it does not acknowledge the disappearance of the place of critique, its critical distance. The postmodern has been interpreted in many ways, but coalesces around notions of loss of depth (critique, meaning, truth, 'metanarrative' in general, affect), play and the crossing of borders between previously discrete genres, cultures, social groupings. In architecture, it may well have a usable, consensual meaning, in that it features references to earlier vernacular(s) and Baudrillard concedes this (*Baudrillard Live*, p. 22). Equally, in art, maybe it can be identified in certain contem-porary practices, and also the insistence on 'where a work is coming from', i.e. the positioning of the artist. Postmodernism supposedly frees us from the constraints of modernism, and all the political and historical violence it emerges with. But Baudrillard's theory does none of the above, and even his disinterestedness is nearer to Sade's 'apathy' than to Jameson's version of anomie. The world Baudrillard sees is not one of breaking down old truths and hierarchies, 'not at all the eclectic and derisory state of postmod-ern indetermination' (*Baudrillard Live*, p. 163), but one of increas-ing auto-control, homogenization rather than diversity in the casual, inane use of 'difference' as positive marker, even though, in a bid to undermine humanist liberal sensibilities, he calls postmod-ernism the first universal, in the form of jeans and Coca-Cola spreading across the world (*Cool Memories II*, p. 70; 268).

Baudrillard does not believe postmodernism has any viability as a conceptual term. He says that 'one should ask whether postmodernism, the postmodern, has a meaning. It doesn't, as far as I am concerned' (*Baudrillard Live*, p. 21), and 'I don't know what a postmodern culture would be' (p. 82). He is actually not interested, and generally only addresses the problem when addressed in interview or dialogue. When pressed, he characterizes what he takes to be postmodern as having largely to do with restoration, rather than reinvention or even pastiche (p. 94).[3] He also refers to the raising up of victimhood, and a focus on an individualism free of content as postmodern (*Illusion*, p. 107; 150). Very occasionally, he seems to bring his own theory within postmodernism, writing, for example, on the postmodern as 'surface', as simulation (*Illusion*, p. 117; 164). This can be seen countered when he claims that the postmodern itself is simulation (*Baudrillard Live*, p. 158), and therefore falls within or beneath his own theory, rather than his theory being a manifestation of it (except insofar as everything in a simulated world is simulated . . .).

We could decide that his view on the postmodern has softened, as shown by his casual use of the term since the early 1990s, and even if it remains occasional, it is often suggestive beyond its immediate textual setting. My own view is that the postmodern is irrelevant to and in Baudrillard because the modern never went away. Many features of postmodernism (fragmentation, play, escape from hierarchies, politicization of art) are resolutely modernist conceits, and if anything, today's postmodernism is a living on in the end of modernism. For Nicholas Zurbrugg, Baudrillard is an example of 'modernist postmodernism'.[4] Baudrillard himself referred to 'us moderns and ultramoderns' (*America*, p. 70; 139), which ties in neatly with Charles Jencks' use of the term ultramodernism to describe 'avant-gardism, deconstruction, silence and minimalism' (*The Language of Postmodern Architecture*, p. 20), where constraining elements of modernism are left behind (notably the epic search for the truth of fragmented reality), but experimentalism still occurs (and is more important than 'play'). In this light, even Baudrillard's playful theorizing in the *Cool Memories* series is not post, but ultra-modern. We can also see this non-postmodernism in Baudrillard's advocacy of all that disrupts postmodern society, and his hope that the homogenization that is properly postmodern will not become total.

Theory

One of the least accurate criticisms that could be made of Baudrillard is that he is complicit with something like a postmodern order, or an apologist for post-capitalist society; Hal Foster suggests 'modern nihilism' as Baudrillard's position, as opposed to a 'resistant' postmodernism (*Postmodern Culture*, p. xv). Baudrillard's observations of simulated, virtual or fractal events and phenomena are in themselves a form of critique, if critique is what you are after. What throws late Marxists is Baudrillard's rejection of critical theory, in favour of a conception of theory where knowledge is not stored, solutions found or truths revealed, whether about ideology or anything else. Theory must no longer even aim for the real, as

> to be the reflection of the real, to enter into a relation of critical negativity with the real cannot be theory's end. This was the pious view of a perpetuated era of Enlightenment, and to this day determines the moral standing of the intellectual. (*Ecstasy*, p. 97; 83)

If the real is gone, theory is wasting its time looking for it, and even more so if it 'finds' it, as this will contribute to hyperrealization, to the replication of the world by itself, as simulation. Critical thought has left us unable to deal with simulation, which is the replacement real we now have (*Impossible Exchange*, p. 18; 29). Theory must be appropriate to its object, and 'must become excessive and sacrificial to speak about excess and sacrifice. It must become simulation if it speaks about simulation, and deploy the same strategy as its object' (*Ecstasy*, p. 98; 84). Georges Bataille could still write about transgression, sacrifice and eroticism in an excessive way, but now even this is gone, and theory might seem excessive, but it must travel within simulation to seem outside it (and seem to be on the inside to get out from it).

Baudrillard offers numerous models for theory, often in conclusion to his collections, and all of which act as a form of challenge or *défi* (ibid.) rather than as confirmation or denial. Theory can be nihilistic – when the real itself is nothing, thought should try to be nothing, should fail (*The Perfect Crime*, p. 151; 207), or even reduce all to nothing, as a form of theoretical terrorism (*Simulacra and Simulation*, p. 163; 233). When theory is nihilist, its purpose is not: in other words, one nihilism exposes another, that of truth, the real, meaning – all of which are constructs. It is a form of deconstruction rather than simple destructiveness.

For this reason, Baudrillard is able to offer more positive, if still odd, versions of what theory should be. In *The Transparency of Evil*, he is keen to present theory as a 'strange attractor': a form that reproduces itself at all levels, around which values (of populations, rainfalls, random numbers) gather and which can also be generated from any chaotic equation. Events are increasingly hard to predict, even if there is a pattern, and 'to capture such strange events, theory itself must be remade as something strange: as a perfect crime, or as a strange attractor' (p. 110; 115). It is not only critique that has disappeared, it is also the referential world and the Subject observer. In their place, we have 'the object as strange attractor [and] the Object is what theory can be for reality: not a reflection, but a challenge, and a strange attractor' (p. 173; 179).

Thought will attract the object through seduction, through appearances, play and putting itself at stake, i.e. in leaving the rational behind. For Baudrillard, seduction is the other to production, the other in the same way difference and, indeed, différance are other to sameness. Production applies to the world of representations, where truths and reality can be uncovered, where the world is real-ized. The world we inhabit as the real world, largely unquestioningly, is one that is fabricated, produced. Seduction, on the other hand, is about appearances, challenge and duel/dual relations. Theory must be seductive, in form and approach (*Impossible Exchange*, pp. 149–51; 186–8). Any new thought must leave humanistic conceptions of morality, truth, knowledge and life alone. Instead it must be inhuman (ibid., p. 24; 36), so we can match the inhuman generated by and in strange attractors. In fact, in thinking the inhuman, we leave our control as subjects behind:

[the] exclusion of the Inhuman [by a society obsessed with human survival, for example] means that from now on it is the Inhuman which

thinks us. We can grasp the world only from an omega point external to the Human, from objects and hypotheses which play, for us, the role of strange attractors. (p. 17; 27)

We seem to have become conduits for a fractal form of seduction, where we theorize aimlessly, as this is the only way anything can be thought without adding to simulation. And yet, there is a positive thought of theory emerging: theory as resistance, as oddness, as continual motion, as replication of simulation without being it, and as the playful polemic Baudrillard's own thought takes. Theory, for Baudrillard, is also subject to qualitative judgement: it must not be critical, it must be seduction, a paradox, or a strange attractor. If the world is paradoxical and uncertain, thought must also be this (*Mots de passe*, p. 101). The last thing we can do is give in to the world around us: 'facing a world that is unintelligible and problematic, our task is clear: we must make that world even more unintelligible, even more enigmatic' (*Vital Illusion*, p. 83). That the real is over (if it ever even was), or that events continue to take place freed of meaning is what drives Baudrillard's thought as it endlessly and gloomily circulates around a morbid real, relentlessly offering counter-realities, resistances and challenges whether we like them or not.

Outline of the book

Baudrillard's early writings were much simpler conceptually, if more onerous to read. They are closer to consensual notions of the social world and how to assess it, even if at times they stray from customary objects of analysis, as in his first book, *The System of Objects*, and seek to work within the tradition of Marxist critique, in parallel with Guy Debord and the Situationists.[5] His approach is essentially the structuralist one, where the meaning of individual moments, objects, words or images occurs within a systematic framework which ultimately defines what they mean through how everything is related. He is also, at least in this first book, quite psychoanalytical in outlook. In *The Consumer Society*, the move from these models is already underway, with Bataille's influence becoming visible. This book is still within the realms of critical discourse, and he was far from alone in dealing with that subject in 1970. Both structuralism and Marxism are unravelled as systems of codification in *For a Critique of the Political Economy of the Sign*, and unceremoniously attacked in *The Mirror of Production*. Gradually, the notion of simulation as the defining characteristic of contemporary society takes hold, and is theorized fully in *Symbolic Exchange and Death*, which is again heavily indebted to Bataille, and also to a perverse use of Freud and Ferdinand de Saussure. The notion of symbolic exchange gradually mutates (from *For a Critique* to *Symbolic Exchange*) from being a possible utopian communication to an always lost absence from societies based on representations. This first period is dealt with in Chapter 1, with the emphasis on how Baudrillard moves from Marxist critique to Bataille, and how symbolic exchange develops from this shift.

From this point on, Baudrillard is interested primarily in what is specific to simulated, hyperreal society (with symbolic exchange its 'other' or what is absent from simulation). He argues that we have only ever had simulacra of one sort or another, and that there has never been a true real that is known to us. Over the course of history, though, we have got further from the realness of symbolic exchange (which maybe we never had) and headed to the 'real world'. There has never been a world realer than ours: everywhere reality is enhanced, multiplied, brought to us, we to it, or is recreated (for the first time) in films or computer games. All of this means we live in a total simulation (although not all the world is there yet). This thought dominates Baudrillard's work, even though, since the early 1990s, he has written of the fractalization of reality, and the virtual that replaces even the thing we thought was reality. The evolution of simulation, in the world and as a concept in Baudrillard, is the subject of Chapter 2.

There is resistance, though, and this takes the form first of all of symbolic exchange, and then of seduction, in the book of the same name. Reality has been produced, been brought into being systematically in the form of representations, meanings and truths, and seduction opposes this, through the play of appearances. Other phenomena (explored in Chapter 3) also act outside, across or against simulation: symbolic violence, the fatal, Evil, illusion and impossible exchange. One of these terms seems always to be at play in Baudrillard, although, as with Derrida, the new term never fully displaces the earlier ones.

Chapter 4 concentrates on what actually happens in a simulated world and looks at Baudrillard's writings on the masses, on terrorism, on reality TV and surveillance, on war, the event, and finally on 9/11. Baudrillard has often been highly controversial, seemingly unwittingly, as with his praise of the masses' 'density'; his writing of America as a 'utopia realized', criticized by those who thought he liked America too much, and others who thought he had totally missed the reality of the country (see the interview in Chapter 6 for Baudrillard's response to that particular criticism); his statements that seemed to criticize the improvement of women's position in society; and perhaps most of all, his writings on the (first) Gulf War (which he says did not happen), and on the destruction of the World Trade Center, where he wrote, in *The Spirit of Terrorism*, of the buildings committing suicide, of the secret glee of us all in seeing them fall, and of how this event is about the only thing that has ever fully resisted simulation, if only momentarily. All of these, however, have a firmer basis than might be believed, and the more outrageous the claim, the more Baudrillard supplies in the way of argument, and, in the case of Gulf wars and 9/11, much of what he has said, along with the *events themselves* have merely followed what he had written long before.

Since the 1980s, most of Baudrillard's books have consisted of articles reunited by a lead essay, which supplies or develops a key concept. The individual pieces often treat very specific events, texts or figures, and Chapter 5 seeks to address themes that have recurred in Baudrillard's readings of contemporary cultural objects. Alongside these collections, Baudrillard has also written regularly for the French daily newspaper *Libération*, and on occasion supplied texts for art exhibitions including his own, for since the mid-1990s, he has been exhibiting his photographs (photography, and also digital media feature in Chapter 5).[6] This less overtly theoretical writing has also found expression in the series of *Cool Memories* books (four so far, spanning twenty years between them). These pseudo-diaries are highly aphoristic, impressionistic texts, which can spend anything from one line to several pages on a topic. They offer a new approach for theoretical writing, in that they do not have the portentousness usually associated with the aphorism. They can be humorous, though, and there is plenty of room for contradictions and sudden shifts. At a more prosaic level, though, they seem to provide the source for whatever books are being written at that time (and Baudrillard is not shy of transposing sections whole).

Chapter 6 is a new interview with Baudrillard, covering many of the issues raised in Chapters 4 and 5, Baudrillard's current theoretical perspectives, and also including a substantial amount of commentary on specific writers and texts (including films such as *The Matrix* and *Minority Report*). Chapter 7 looks at key influences on Baudrillard, notably Bataille, Marshall McLuhan, J.G. Ballard, Elias Canetti, Friedrich Nietzsche, and the events of 1968. Baudrillard has in turn informed the work of Arthur Kroker and areas of contemporary art, despite his work resisting appropriation. The conclusion closes the book with a brief consideration of a term that has recently taken on some importance in Baudrillard. This is the notion of 'singularity', which stands both in and outside of simulation, and represents a transformation of the density of the masses into a density of specific events, such that they resist incorporation into simulation and/or critical analysis.

Notes

1. Here is a small sample from that realm: Mike Featherstone writes that 'Baudrillard is certainly one of the most extreme of the academic writers in pushing the logic of postmodernism as far as it will go' (*Consumer Culture and Postmodernism*, p. 33); for Steven Connor, in Baudrillard, we see the collapse of the idea of the social 'at its most extreme' (*Postmodernist Culture*, p. 61); for Best and Kellner, Baudrillard 'was crowned as the high priest of the new epoch' and has produced 'the most striking and extreme theory of postmodernism yet produced' (*Postmodern Theory*, p. 111). No survey, however minimal, would be complete without Norris's unfathomably influential derision: Baudrillard, for Norris, is 'the most extreme instance of the "postmodern" drive to extend the aesthetic (i.e. the realm of imaginary representations) to the point of collapsing every

form of ontological distinction or critical truth-claim' (*What's Wrong with Postmodernism*, p. 23). This relatively reasonable, if inaccurate statement will later give way to the impatience of the following: Baudrillard is 'a cult figure on the current "postmodernist" scene, and purveyor of some of the silliest ideas yet to get a hearing among disciples of French intellectual fashion' (*Uncritical Theory*, p. 11).

2. At this point, the literal-minded Sokal and Bricmont might pounce, saying this is not how black holes work, that a black hole isn't even a metaphor (they do not understand that any description is metaphor, particularly of such inaccessible objects), and that the non-scientist has no right to the non-metaphor anyway.

3. See also *Cool Memories* (p. 171; 151), where postmodernity is thought of as retroactive, and also *Illusion* (p. 27; 47), where today's interest in recycling rubbish signals the more pervasive sense of recycling of the postmodern period (as in the rebirth of atavistic politics, for example, or in the insistence on repentance, notably at the international political level (p. 35; 58). The recycling can also be taken more abstractly as the recycling of forms (*Paroxysm*, p. 109; 194). See Gane, *In Radical Uncertainty* (p. 31–2), on Baudrillard's view of the postmodern.

4. See for example, 'Baudrillard, Modernism and Postmodernism', in Kellner (ed.), *Baudrillard: A Critical Reader* (pp. 229–55).

5. For an overview of how the various currents of thought emerge and interrelate, post-1968, see Keith A. Reader, *Intellectuals and the Left in France since 1968*.

6. This is not Baudrillard's first foray into the production of art objects. In 1978, he published a short poetic book, *L'Ange de stuc* (English version, *The Stucco Angel*, in *The Uncollected Baudrillard*, Genosko (ed.), pp. 78–90).

Chapter 1

System and Exchange:
From Marxism to the Symbolic

Structures of contemporary society

Baudrillard's work has often been categorized as having a 'before and after', in terms of a break with Marxism. This can be variously dated, but the latest it occurs is the appearance of *Symbolic Exchange and Death* in 1976, where the Marxism dissipates. Any reading would have to concede that Baudrillard's first four books feature Marxist ideas heavily, even if his is a cultural, less than dogmatic Marxism. But once we go beyond a schematic regard, other problematics occur so early on, that with hindsight, the emphasizing of Marxism should be reduced. I believe Baudrillard authorizes us to do this, when making the following retrospective injunction as to the status of his œuvre:

> One must pretend that the œuvre pre-existed itself, and knew of its end from the beginning . . . Yet, in this there is an exercise in simulation that can open up resonances with one of the principal themes of the whole: pretending that the œuvre is complete, that it developed in a coherent manner, that it had always existed. Therefore, I see no way of speaking about it, other than in terms of simulation. (*Ecstasy*, pp. 9–10; 9)

The simulation here is double: first, the œuvre itself is a simulation, reconstructed as if every text were always somehow already present. Second, simulation as an idea is at the centre of Baudrillard's work, being introduced as early as 1976. In this chapter, then, 'early Baudrillard' is seen abandoning Marxism, and other 'economic' theories, such as Bataille's notion of the general economy, take its place, and inform Baudrillard's other central idea – that of symbolic exchange. The relation between these two terms is laid out in *Symbolic Exchange*.

As well as Marxism, this 'early' period can be characterized as being structuralist, and, initially at least, strongly influenced by psychoanalysis. Rather than seeing a split between acceptance and rejection, I think we can read this phase as being one of gradual dismantling. Baudrillard appears to work his way out of these as dominant problematics (although in the case of psychoanalysis, this is characterized, initially, as more of a shift from Freud to Lacan). If Baudrillard accepts these ideas as thoroughly historicized (more products of their time than comments on it) and, by the mid-1970s, as finished, then the reader should, to an extent, at least, follow this.

If the above are perspectives that Baudrillard considers he has dealt with, then what are the aspects that emerge in their place? – primarily the symbolic, particularly in the form of symbolic exchange (as distinctly opposed to Lacan's conception of the Symbolic); and the problem of the status of the real. A point that must be made is that when Baudrillard 'completes' the analysis of a subject, whether it be 'consumption' or 'Marx', it is not always clear if he has retained aspects of it or entirely dismissed it. It is also difficult, as early as *Symbolic Exchange*, to identify Baudrillard's position and whether he has any critical perspective on the phenomena he identifies as important.

In the case of the first two books, *The System of Objects* and *The Consumer Society*, exhaustive, critical studies are made of aspects of modern society (that may or may not define it as a whole). At this stage, Baudrillard is well within the confines of (Marxist) sociology, but with the addition of structuralism and psychoanalysis, which are central concerns of the human sciences at that time. It is ironic, given that reliance on prevailing ideologies, that *System* and its successor offer the only occasion of Baudrillard entertaining a largely unproblematic relation with objectivity. These first two books question knowable objects, whereas later on it is the Object world and our attempts to know it that are questioned, to the extent that the Object turns on us, or alternatively loses itself, along with the Subject, in simulation.

In *System*, Baudrillard attempts to explain our relation with the objects that surround us, and that come to define us. He does not merely catalogue objects, but seeks the process whereby we 'live' objects and how they come to respond to needs which are other than functional. All of this takes place in a 'cultural system', in combination with 'mental structures' (*System*, p. 4; 9). In terms of theory, the important elements are semiotics as a development of structural linguistics, Freudian psychoanalysis and Marxism, and the now less used theories of consumer society (Veblen, Packard). None of these formulations is at all questioned in the course of this text (except the last, and this only gently), but later texts, perhaps precisely for this reason, will lay all of these open for extensive criticism.

The objects in question cannot be separated from the system. This system is one of meaning, of signification, rather than one of triumphal technological items which solve problems for an independent subject (which is a discourse generated by the system itself). So the way we come to understand objects is through being able to locate the individual speech act (*parole*) of an object, within the various encodings of the 'language' of objects (p. 10; 17). An object does retain a real function, however – except in the case of meta- or non-functional objects – even if 'for any object . . . the reality principle may be put in brackets' (p. 117; 165).[1] Baudrillard covers this with structural linguistics' differentiation between two levels of meaning: denotation and connotation. Here, the first of these terms would apply to an object's function, and the second to its acquired cultural meaning. Baudrillard adds that these are not 'totally separable' (p. 10 translation modified; 16) – a view he will later challenge.[2] An object can present a 'strict functionality' as a connotation – which is not to say it is not efficient, but that the levels of meaning have infiltrated each other (for example, high grade stereo equipment makes a point of having the minimum display of functions – not solely for efficiency, but also to connote it).

At the same time, everything becomes connotation. Nature becomes naturality (pp. 56–7; 80), function becomes functionality (pp. 63–5; 89–91). Functionality is the lynchpin of the system: 'Every object claims to be functional, just as every regime claims to be democratic' (p. 63; 89). It is this capacity on the part of an object that gives it its place in the system. The 'system' lives on the notion that the consumer-subject has choice, and genuine freedom in that choice. Advertising represents (literally) the irruption of this 'freedom', as we are all given advertising, so it is democratic (p. 171; 239), and we all have the possibility of placing ourselves according to our choice of brands. The ideology of freedom of choice is further maintained by the targeting of specific groups by particular advertisers, and further promulgated in, for example, specialist magazines or websites. As Baudrillard was writing his analyses of consumer society in the late 1960s, the appeal to consumers that imagine themselves to be 'different' was less pronounced than today (he mentions 'personalization' of objects, but the massive incorporation of 'alternatives' offered by subcultures had yet to occur). On the question of brands, however, what he says is relevant: he argues that 'brand loyalty' is a highly impoverished language: all it 'says' is I stick to this brand: it is a self-contained message (pp. 191–2; 267–8). There are many possibilities of subverting the world of corporate imposition of identities, but it is very hard to not pay the companies anyway, at which point they don't care how subversive you think you are.

The implication is that there has been a real, natural world which has been steamrollered into 'culture', as 'the whole world thus becomes integrated as spectacle in the domestic universe' (p. 43; 59). This quotation is specifically used by Baudrillard with regard to glass, but certainly seems to sum up the position Baudrillard takes on the systematization of modern culture (in which *System* is complicit).

This nostalgic position is not made explicit as Baudrillard is not totally against progress, but objects to its distortions under capitalism. Humanity (or 'Man' as Baudrillard refers to it) has disposed of its traditional link with objects – a link that is symbolic due to the direct working of an object, rather than the distance of control. This is the process whereby 'man evolves to an objective social becoming' (p. 48 trans. mod.; 67). Baudrillard sees automation, and the distance that arrives through an increase in push button control as opposed to direct use, as being the development most indicative of this process (and eventually we become operators within the machine that is our house, 'functional' occupants (p. 27; 37)).

There is confusion throughout *System* as to when this process started. At times it may be the arrival of culture in the first place (pp. 64–5; 91), with nature becoming 'Nature' and other to culture. At others it may be the arrival of the capitalist era, or the consumer society, or a conflation of the two.[3] This conflation is justified by Baudrillard in the familiar Marxist formulation of modes of production as defining the historical reality of any society and/or its development: 'The relation of Man to object is subjected to a social dialectic which is that of the forces of production' (p. 48; 68, trans. my own).[4] At a later stage Baudrillard dates the birth of the object system to the Bauhaus, where 'the possibility of a "universal semiotic of technological experience" is in effect born of the abolition of the segregation between the beautiful and the useful' (*For a Critique*, p. 186; 231). As a result, objects, 'once functionally liberated, [they] begin to make themselves signs' (p. 190 trans. mod.; 236–7), and this supposedly represented a radical move. He does not make the claim that this could happen solely because of developments in the domain of ideas or of conscious individual practice, but that it marked the development of the combination of material production and sign production. Which of these preceded the other is never clarified, and in these early works, we are often left without a sense of causality, even though it would be useful to the projects Baudrillard undertakes.

In addition to the role played by the 'forces of production' and the systematization of signs, there is the role of the unconscious to take into account. In *System*, Baudrillard gives us what can only be described as vulgar Freudianism, free of any worry as to its fundamental truth. The unconscious is a simple set of clearly defined vectors, it is universal (i.e. ahistorical) and mediates our perception of the products of our 'social dialectic'. There is 'a collusion . . . somewhere between the collective order of production and an individual order of needs, albeit an unconscious one' (p. 128; 181). As Kellner notes, Baudrillard never decides whether one of these predominates – 'which is the motor behind the proliferation of the new world of objects' (*Baudrillard*, p. 11). While this is a reasonable comment, it also serves as double evidence of the Marxian approach espoused by Kellner: first, that there must be a dominant explanation, a 'last instance'. This should be class-based economy, but if not, at least there should be a recognizable determining factor. Second, there should be some sort of agency, a specified site where we could intervene to change things.

It is nonetheless the case that *System* suffers from a lack of (historical) movement: the sign system has to have appeared more or less complete at some moment; the unconscious is absolute and unchangeable, and in this combination the forms that productive society has taken appear totally arbitrary. In *System*, even the combination of various 'causal' factors produces only a static, functionalist view of society.

Baudrillard's move to the symbolic, which accumulates through succeeding texts to its culmination in *Symbolic Exchange*, serves to highlight the deficiencies of his approach to psychoanalysis in *System*.[5] Baudrillard's Freudianism is more dogmatic than Freud's – objects are phallic (e.g. cars) or uterine (bowls, etc.) and the entire enterprise rests on the male subject being the possessor of the unconscious. It is resolutely phallocentric. This can best be illustrated by the problems Baudrillard encounters around the area of fetishism.[6] Baudrillard notes that a sexual preference which centres on a particular part of a woman's body renders her into an object or objects to be collected (*System*, pp. 99–100; 141). It is clear that there is to be no question of who will be the subject and who the object in this relation. This is confirmed later, when Baudrillard tells us that 'that which has a sex resists fragmenting projection' (p. 101; 143). Woman has never been a subject in possession of a sex, so cannot resist such a de-sexualizing operation, whereas Baudrillard's Man can never be fetishized. This is taken by Baudrillard to be a totally natural phenomenon, rather than a part of the phallocentrism that constitutes the unified (male) Subject, as writers such as Luce Irigaray would argue. Baudrillard's definition of the fetish as something 'equivalent to the penis' (p. 101n; 143n) also becomes problematic – if we are talking about an object for the gratification of the 'perverse auto-erotic system' (p. 101; 142), surely this would be threatened by another 'active agent'. In any case, Freud is not so certain on this point: 'The shoe or slipper is a (corresponding) symbol of the *female* genitals' (Freud, *Essentials of Psychoanalysis*, p. 299n).[7] I do not wish to dwell on fetishism in the clinical sense, as Baudrillard's later writings re-introduce the more interesting form – the fetish as imbued with spirit, or *mana*. His problems with the psychoanalytic category of fetishism stem as much from the reductionism of psychoanalysis as from the deficiencies of his own view.[8]

Although there is a largely unquestioning use of psychoanalytic jargon and assertion ('authenticity always stems from the Father' (*System*, p. 77; 108)), Baudrillard does start moving to a notion that the unconscious is structured around, and perhaps because of, lack and death. This is mainly evident in the analysis of collection (pp. 85–106; 120–50), which centres on the notion that a collection is not designed to be complete – the missing term is death (p. 92; 130); and in the closing section announcing the next phase of the Baudrillard œuvre ('Towards a definition of consumption' (pp. 199–205; 275–83)) where he suggests that consumer society is our way of formally (i.e. apparently) resolving our internal conflicts that stem from lack. That is why there are no limits to consumption (p. 204; 282). This apparent resolution is what perpetuates alienation. The 'system of objects' gives us a way of placing ourselves in a stratified – but not fixed – bourgeois society: 'the code produces an illusion of transparency, an illusion of readable social relations, behind which the real structure of production and real social relationships remain illegible' (p. 196; 274). As usual, structuralism seeks a semiotics that emerges whole from the structural relations of items, but ends up providing external rationalizations.

In *Consumer*, Baudrillard extends his analysis to the societal logic that operates the system of objects. The consumer society is not one where we are all simply forced to consume what we do not need, rather, it is 'the way our society speaks itself'. And, in a sense, the only objective reality of consumption is the *idea* of consumption (*Consumer*, p. 193; 311–12). What we are consuming is the notion of consumption as a whole, as being the normal operational logic of society, rather than 'goods' as such. Baudrillard is targeting the individual's relation to the object, 'no longer relating to a particular object in its specific utility, but to a set of objects in its total signification' (p. 27; 20). The person here refers to 'the consumer', and therefore this quotation undermines claims for there being such a thing as needs that would exist independently from the system of consumption and signification. What is at stake is not 'commodities' as individual commodities, as such a concept could have no independent meaning (although 'commodity form' would be relatively near), but the system which allows and regulates both the idea of the commodity, and its circulation, that is, the sign system that 'consumption' represents.

The link from *System* is accomplished via the notion of personalization, which is a crucial notion within *Consumer*. In the earlier work, personalization is attained through acquiring 'marginally different' products (i.e. different colours, brands, levels of sophistication); which then identify us as an individual (*System*, pp. 141–3; 198–9). Baudrillard extends this to its conclusion to say that the Subject has been dismissed, to be spuriously reconstituted via 'personalized' objects (*Consumer*, p. 88; 125), and that therefore the 'singularity' of the person is lost (p. 88; 126).[9] This is a result of our processes of differentiation, which for Baudrillard is partly an essential social fact, which he argues Galbraith, for example, neglects (p. 74; 102); and partly a system introduced by the 'forces of production', i.e. an ideology of individualism, rather than individuality. Therefore, while the main drive to differentiation may be 'falsely' induced in capitalism, there is already a psychic predisposition which is implicitly, for Baudrillard, the founding instance of society.

It is this combination of rationales for differentiation that institutes the system of signs whereby different aspects or quantities of 'knowledge', 'possessions' or '(high) culture' can define our status and relative grouping (p. 54; 68). Consumer society is not, for Baudrillard, a 'self-integrating, class-differentiated social structure' as Gane puts it (*Bestiary*, p. 70). Hierarchy can and does persist, and growth is a function of the system for maintaining its inequalities (*Consumer*, p. 53; 67), but the vital aspect is one of perceived freedom and mobility that arises when all can be bought (p. 61; 79–80) and that differentiation is unlimited (p. 62; 81). In no way can the logic of consumer society admit to class-based differences, although members of a group may perceive (or be led to perceive) that possession of certain items will define them as being members of a given class.

Baudrillard does perceive these systems of difference, equality, freedom, etc. as being ideological. They are devices used to maintain the 'actual relations of production'. Consumer society 'frees' people to be consumers in the same way nineteenth-century capitalism freed people to be workers. This is developed when Baudrillard talks of credit as a means of disciplining society – exhorted to consume, the work must follow (pp. 81–3; 114–18). There is also an ideology of the gift – in the shop window display (p. 166; 264), sales (p. 164; 261), and advertising (*System*, pp. 164–96; 229–54), which offers the illusion of total, equal access to the products and concurrent signification of the system.[10]

Sexual difference is given significance in consumerism, with advertising codes taking up earlier characterizations of male and female genders. Men are exhorted to compete with each other, while women are to treat themselves as objects for display (*Consumer*, pp. 96–7; 140–1). This cementing of already constructed gender identities, is, nonetheless, too readily accepted by Baudrillard, as can be seen when he refers to the female consumer, who '"consumes" culture, though she does not even do this in her own right: it is decorative culture' (p. 98; 142). While Baudrillard is not wrong in how women are placed within consumerism, here his position is a reiteration of Baudelaire (all too directly, given the gap of over one hundred years), and also denies any agency within those codes (see Baudelaire, *The Painter of Modern Life*).

Kellner emphasizes Baudrillard's use of a 'much more explicit Marxian framework' (*Baudrillard*, p. 14), but Marxism is already implicitly becoming part of the problem, and marginalized in the multiple determinations beyond the economic or the political. Kellner neglects a major, specifically economic aspect of Baudrillard's formulation of the 'ideology of consumer society', that of abundance, which brings into play a critique of the progress that society has apparently made. Gane, on the other hand, is keen to show Baudrillard as being highly critical of consumerism in its own right. In looking at the conclusion of *Consumer*, he argues that we are moving 'towards a pact with the devil' that loses our soul and leads to alienation in consumer society (*Bestiary*, pp. 71–4). Baudrillard writes precisely the opposite, that the pact with the devil no longer offers a meaningful representation as we see 'the individual not as alienated substance, but as shifting difference, this novel process, which is not analyzable in terms of the person' (*Consumer*, p. 193; 311).

Alienation, as well as transcendence, is lost, and although

Baudrillard does not see this as positive, mentioning the 'void of human relations' (p. 196; 316), or their 'atrocity' (p. 162; 258), he largely accepts this as a process that has occurred, and that any restorable, preferable state will have to refer to ambivalence rather than to a more accurate and clear definition (based on, for example, ideological critique), which is itself a ruse of modern (rationalist) society. What, then, has been lost, or obscured, for Baudrillard, in the processes of capitalist consumer society?

There are several important elements which cause *Consumer* to diverge from Marxism, and these will take on increased importance in his succeeding works. The first of these is the notion of abundant society. Both 'bourgeois' and Marxist theory subscribe to the concept that society has advanced and will continue to advance to greater prosperity and equality (whether this occurs 'within' society or as a result of a nation being 'ripe for revolution', whether through wealth or the proletariat's awareness of their 'right' to it, is irrelevant). Baudrillard does insist that equality/inequality is a difference determined ideologically within the 'democratic system'. In other words, capitalism rationalizes and universalizes a process of hierarchization that is always at work, but was previously less efficient: 'the capitalist system (and the productivist system in general) has been the culmination of that functional unlevelling, that disequilibrium, by rationalizing it and generalizing it in all respects' (*Consumer*, p. 53; 66).[11] Equally, rights are not an 'objective social progress' (p. 58; 75), they only come into play as the facility to engage in a given act comes under threat, and in some sense no longer exist from the moment they are called 'rights'.

This is an extension of Marshall Sahlins' questioning of the so-called 'abundance' of modern Western society. Sahlins' conception is that ours is a society of scarcity, of affluence rather than abundance. Societies of the 'hunter-gatherer' type, for example, experience abundance despite being 'objectively poor'. In these societies, it is impossible to monopolize resources and nature is seen as providing sufficient resources, no matter what the level. Needs do not exist, as a category, until resources are controlled, so we cannot talk of 'real' or 'false' needs (*Consumer*, pp. 125–6; 193–6). Need is founded on a lack, and therefore insatiable.

There can be no definition of a need, if there is no fulfilment (p. 78; 108).

In a major recasting of his conception of psychoanalysis, Baudrillard states that any apparent increase in sexual liberties is only in the domain 'of signs, not of meaning' (p. 148; 233). Where before he saw phallic, oral, anal connotations everywhere, he now criticizes 'vaudeville Freudianism' (p. 149; 235, trans. my own). Everyone has been 'given the right' to their unconscious, but all this consists of is a tautological proof by the existence of 'its' own reproduced symbols. These 'symbols' are induced by psychoanalysis, and are signs of the functioning of psychoanalysis (p. 147; 233). This is, in fact, the censure of the genuine symbolic, in favour of the symbolic function and 'the denial of sexuality as symbolic exchange' (p. 149; 237). The symbolic (Baudrillard's version) is unattainable in representation, because 'the true fantasy is unrepresentable. If it *could* be represented, it would be unbearable' (p. 148 trans. mod.; 234).

What we have, particularly as a result of psychoanalysis, is a movement (away from the symbolic) which parallels the movement to economic exchange. 'Primitive' societies do not have 'access' to a symbolic, but *inhabit* it through the ambivalence of exchange which is not one of fixed values, separate from its enactors. This loss of the symbolic dimension (replaced with a signifying symbolic) emphasizes the real world, to the cost of anything else, including distance from this apparently real world (dominated by ideology, of 'living in the real world', and conforming). Ironically, though, the real becomes less and less real as a result of this triumph.

The constant barrage of news – the production of the real world – is a crucial part of consumption; we are increasingly exhorted to know what is going on in the 'real world', which is itself a construct that emanates from the media. As with needs, rights and exchange, the 'real world' is only called into play as its realness recedes: 'what mass communications give us is not reality, but the dizzying whirl of the real' (p. 34; 32). Events are rendered banal by their repetition, their enclosure in the media form, and the 'cruel exteriority of the world becomes something intimate and warm' (p. 35; 34). This is aided and abetted by the levelling out of information, with the cycle of news/fiction/advertising nullifying the power of events to disturb.[12] In a final manoeuvre, contemporary society has managed also to excise the world's ambivalent, dangerous nature, in the consumption of the real via televised news. This is a process, Baudrillard suggests, that all the processes of rational Western society are engaged in: real-ization leading to loss of the symbolic.

The essential tool that has diverted 'nature' into 'naturality', reality into realism, symbolic exchange into economic/rational exchange is the system of signs by which all has become objectifiable, codifiable. This, combined with the forces of production, is seen by Baudrillard to be the defining factor of Western industrial/rational society, hence the perceived virtues of analyses based on structural linguistics and/or historical materialism. What has been up to now acceptance with points of tension turns into problematization, as Baudrillard now moves on to the interrogation of signs and political economy, and the complicity of those systems of thought based on them. Charles Levin writes that Baudrillard's 'appropriation of structuralism . . . is . . . an act of aggression that virtually destroys its object' ('Introduction', p. 11), which he could equally have written of Baudrillard's use of Marxism.[13]

Dismantling Marxist logic

Several of the essays that make up *For a Critique* are contemporaneous with *System* and *Consumer*, and merely reiterate or rehearse formulations that are expanded on in these texts. As the title suggests, the prime concern of the 'text' as far as its not altogether matched components can be said to have just one (or even one), is to develop a theory that combines a critique of political economy (whether 'bourgeois' or Marxist) with one of the sign (whether its functioning or analysis in structural linguistics), and to thus fabricate a critique that can speak of a generalized political economy.

We are led into this critique through a problematization of 'fetishism'. This has become a lazy term, writes Baudrillard, and also contains moral overtones, whereby one set of beliefs is deemed false (*For a Critique*, pp. 88–9; 95–6). According to Baudrillard, fetishism is for Marx the interiorization of the 'generalized system of exchange value' (p. 88; 95), which, for Baudrillard, presupposes a potential real state away from exchange value. Any supposed hold that objects may have comes only from a system of signs, therefore an 'alienated subject' would not be fetishizing the signifier, but the signified, or the possibility of such a thing being true (p. 92; 100). This is the realm of ideology – the spread of the code which wishes to present the possibility of a hidden 'real content' – a trap which Marxism can and does fall prey to. The exchange value of signs induces, rather than hiding or obscuring, use value, and the 'absolute condition for [its] ideological functioning is the loss of the symbolic and the passing over to the semiological' (p. 98; 109).[14] It is only hinted at later, but Baudrillard seems to suggest that desire has forced us to codify, to eliminate its uncertainties: 'desire has little vocation to fulfilment in "liberty", but rather in the rule – not the transparency of a value content, but in the opacity of the code of value' (p. 209; 264). It seems, then, that the mechanisms of the modern Subject are geared precisely to allay the symbolic. It is possible that all society has, for Baudrillard, attempted this, but ours is the most constraining. If there is alienation, it is to an extent because we want it. Once again, fetishism is problematized in its usage as 'inferior or false perception'. Nonetheless, it also appears that Baudrillard is offering us a universal fetishism wherein signs are everything. As a result, our belief in any reality behind (within) the sign could be seen as 'ontological fetishism', in a way that begins to suggest Baudrillard's move to simulation. At this stage of Baudrillard's writings, the question for the reader arises as to what existence the symbolic might have had, before the 'arrival' of sign systems, because we certainly seem to have lost some form of unmediated existence. Maybe it, too, was only conceived of when its 'reality' was inaccessible. Its positioning on the 'outside' is stressed throughout *For a Critique*, and is even summed up in a formula, which posits an equivalence between the unities of the sign (signifier/signified) and the commodity (exchange value/use value), with this equivalence opposed by symbolic exchange (p. 128; 152). This systematic reduction, however, places the symbolic firmly in the system of meaning – if only to counteract it. Perhaps the ambivalence of symbolic exchange has always introduced a supplement.

   From fetishism, Baudrillard moves on to a critique of the notion of use value, as found in Marx and his successors. Baudrillard claims that, for Marx, use value is separable from exchange value, and that commodity X would always be seen to be useful for task X, with or without generalized exchange value (p. 130; 154). According to Foley, however, for Marx, 'without commodity exchange the usefulness of products in general is a fact self-evident and thus invisible to producers and users' (Bottomore, *A Dictionary of Marxist Thought*, p. 505). In other words, use value is meaningless without exchange value, and this is something Baudrillard's critique could have recognized. Baudrillard continues where perhaps he should have started – stating that 'utility itself – is a fetishized *social relation* just like the abstract equivalence of commodities' (*For a Critique*, p. 131; 155). It is what constitutes use value that counts (the idea of a true utility), and which has been neglected, through the '[abstraction] of the system of needs cloaked in the false evidence of a concrete destination and purpose, an intrinsic finality of goods and products' (ibid.).

If exchange value abstracts 'real labour', then utility itself is a systemized abstraction of equivalence too. It is the combination of these that forms a commodity fetishism. Baudrillard then reverses what we have taken to be Marx's position, and argues that the *notion* of utility must precede generalizable exchange, as there would not otherwise be exchange value. So we did not move from pure use to use value/exchange value in the commodity; rather, it is labour and use value that are the site of fetishism. In Marx, this is the residue of the analysis of the commodity, which 'is a use-value or object of utility, and a "value" . . . distinct from its natural form' (*Capital*, vol. I, p. 152). In other words, the 'natural form' is the 'being as object'. This true form, and the true relation we should have with each other, will be revealed only when the commodity-based world of capitalism disappears (p. 173). Meanwhile, if use value is only an effect of exchange value, as Marxists would have it ('commodities must be realised as values before they can be realised as use-values' (*Capital*, vol. I, p. 179)), then we cannot talk of a 'liberation of needs' (*For a Critique*, p. 139; 164). Baudrillard does qualify his criticism in writing that perhaps only now can we have this perspective on 'real needs', with the advent of consumer society (p. 135; 162), wherein 'real needs' are not as fixed as before. This acknowledges that Marx was right but only for his time, in this respect at least. In the same way that the commodity has to be analysed in both its terms, so must the sign, as it has suffered the same 'second level fetishism', that is, fetishism of a 'real' component and a 'false' one. The signifier is seen as a general value of exchange, while the signified has been left as a real content. Structuralism problematizes this, but just wheels in the referent as a real externality to be signified.[15]

Baudrillard has demonstrated what he takes to be a homology between the sign and political economy; they have the same form and it is *this* form that 'describes the field of general political economy' (p. 127; 149). This form shows that ideology follows the logic that splits into two terms and creates one apparently real level, and an equivalent apparently false one. The process of ideology is the imposition of value, reducing possibilities and removing all 'symbolic ambivalence' (p. 149; 181). Even with a plurality of different possible signifiers, '*equivalence* has simply become *polyvalence*' (p. 150 trans. mod.; 181). Ambivalence, though, would 'solve the equation'. Ambivalence is in some way the 'natural' for Baudrillard here, as we are told that reality is the horizon of the sign: the sign tries to capture the real and never can, which is why it must pursue 'the detour of the real' (p. 154; 187) that is the referent. Natural, but not real in any useful sense, as signification does not dispose of the real, but of the symbolic, as signs are always positive (convey meaning), whereas 'the symbolic is not [a] value. It is loss, resolution of value and of the positivity of the sign' (p. 161; 196).[16] The real is a 'simulacrum of the symbolic' (p. 162; 198), and our thoughts of revolution must turn to the restitution of the symbolic: 'The signs too, must burn' (p. 163 trans. mod.; 199).

Baudrillard is leaving Marxism's comforting clutches, but still pictures a radicality – one of the restoration of the symbolic – not through set actions, but through risk, loss, defiance of the value system and where 'jouissance is *radical*' (p. 207 trans. mod.; 261), as opposed to value, which sublimates jouissance.[17] In this move, consummation (*consumation*) replaces consumption (*consommation*), in a radical re-orientation towards general economy:

Consummation [consumation] (play, gift, destruction as pure loss, symbolic reciprocity) attacks the code itself, breaks it, deconstructs it.

The symbolic act is the destruction of the value code (exchange and use) not the destruction of objects in themselves. Only this act can be termed 'concrete', since it alone breaks and transgresses the abstraction of value. (p. 135n; 161n)[18]

May 1968 witnessed some possible variants on the restoration of the symbolic, but often not in the guise of what were termed symbolic acts: for example, taking over the media, because the circuits of communication were not disrupted *in their form*. In this case, it was still clear who was the sender of the message (pp. 169–70; 208–9). This is the problem with the 'medium become message': not that it transmits ideology, but that its form is ideological. The diffusion of 'symbolic acts' on television became their confirmation; their reproducibility their medium (p. 174; 215) because they just used a tool complicit in the dissemination of the (exchange) values of consumer society, and as a result the symbolic aspect vanished. Genuinely symbolic acts of May 1968 were such things as graffiti, street encounters, 'immediate inscription' (p. 176; 218), although this seems weak in terms of Baudrillard's own argument, or as a means of bringing social change, which he later comes to recognize.

Marx and Marxian analysis have served Baudrillard's analysis, and he often claims to be building on, rather than writing against, Marx's logic. Nonetheless, there remains a final, and crucial, stumbling block in Marxism, and this prevents him from being 'neo-Marxian'. The hints of problems with Marxism had already gone back to Marx with Baudrillard's critique of the unquestioned nature of utility. In *Mirror*, this expands through the concept of labour into the problematization of production as a category. For Baudrillard, there is a fundamental lack of analysis, whether in Marx, or by Marxists, of production *per se*. Due to its universalization as a category, if there is a problem with the category of production, the whole Marxist project is jeopardized and always has been.

Production has been taken to mean material production: this is both where Marxism comes in, and where its analysis goes. Economic freedom is supposed to initiate 'real' freedom. How different is this from 'bourgeois economics', asks Baudrillard

(*Mirror*, pp. 17–18; 18–21). Following on from the reconceptualiza-
tion of use value in *For a Critique*, Baudrillard notes that for economic material production to be either the 'motor for change' or
'freedom', there must be something seen to be concrete 'useful'
work, something which is progressively liberated as History
reaches its endpoint. The workforce is seen as 'abstract social
labour plus concrete labour' (*Mirror*, p. 20; 23) and it is the
exchange value/abstraction of labour which prevents the freedom
of labour. Baudrillard, however, asserts that the 'usefulness' of generalized labour (as category) must precede exchange value: a particular piece of work is not intrinsically useful, but it is seen to be,
and can therefore be generalized as 'labour'. This is opposed to the
Marxist conception whereby labour (as objective category) is alienated from its product. Therefore, argues Baudrillard, it is Marxism,
just as much as 'bourgeois economics', that keeps capitalism going.
As anarchists have long argued, work does not make us free.[19]

Marxism takes the workings of capitalism, in the form of pro-
ductivism, and exports them throughout cultures, history and the
future. In this universalization, Marxism spreads the word that is
the 'ideology of the system' (p. 31; 33). Is this just a 'vulgar'
Marxism? Baudrillard argues that even 'advanced' Marxism
requires production as its *raison d'être*; all it has done is spread the
logic of material production into culture or the psyche. Where it
may suggest otherwise, it merely reproduces a 'bourgeois' idealism
as a superstructure for 'real material conditions' (pp. 32, 35–7; 34,
37–9). The concept of History is historical, and production is a
product (p. 47; 48). On the one hand, Marx could not write differently, as a writer at a specific historical conjuncture, on the other,
for Baudrillard, it is Marx's formulations that make this conceptualization possible. Fundamentally, according to Baudrillard,
theory and its object cannot surpass each other – they spiral in an
'unsurpassable specularity' (p. 29 trans. mod.; 27).[20] And this is not
just any theory, but the functioning of a theory which consists of a
doubling of the subject in the specularity of production.

The self is produced in this relation: all *subjects* must exhibit their
relation to the individual in the mirror of production. We are
placed in a vast societal version of Lacan's mirror stage, where the
subject comes to *be* through recognition in the mirror (p. 12; 19).

As it is production that defines the subject, the subject must be produced, through his labour, and 'man becomes his own signified'
(ibid.). He is, therefore, a fixable value, as part of the circuits of
exchange and use, form and content. According to Baudrillard, all
of this implies that we are entrapped precisely where we seek
freedom, since we have no conception of the arena of symbolic
exchange that other societies inhabit. This annuls Marxism's conception of history as the progress of modes of production produc-
ing historicized individuals, as 'there is neither a *mode of production
nor production* in primitive societies, and in primitive societies, there
is *no dialectic* and *no unconscious*' (p. 49 trans. mod.; 49). If this is the
case, then history as teleological progress is invalidated, and as a
result, even the Marxist analysis of 'modern' society is invalid.

It is for this reason that the operation of pre- and non-capitalist
societies must be turned on our society as critique (ibid.). In fact, it
is not only capitalist rationalism that has sought to universalize, as
several religions have also done so, and the 'Judaeo-Christian'
inheritance of Western capitalist society was the first to enact the
profound break between Man and Nature: the former as user, the
latter as resource to be worked. This is the end of 'magical immersion' that appears in most other religions (p. 67; 63). Personal salvation is a process of work, to be attained by certain specified
means (p. 68; 64). The Enlightenment followed, giving birth to
Nature, as the supreme referent, and to nature as a potentiality of
forces. The Subject is broken from Object/Nature (p. 56; 54).
Marxists have never questioned the naturalness or otherwise of
this Nature, or of production as response to needs, or that nature
be worked for this satisfaction of needs (p. 59; 56).

When Marxism[21] attempts its teleology of social development,
it cannot but fail, within its limits. Primitive societies are subsistence economies, we are told. For Baudrillard, this is a moral, not
an economic judgement (i.e. they have produced just enough) and
does not comprehend a 'system' without producers, equivalence,
needs, etc. (pp. 81–2; 74–5). Equally moralistic is the view that they
could have a surplus if they did not 'waste' it in celebrations (*fêtes*).
Symbolic exchange does not differentiate 'goods' for 'use', as all
are part of the process of reciprocal exchange, and work is within
magic and nature (and their exchanges). Marxism takes the sym-

bolic in these societies and makes it an aspect to be excised in the heroic journey to rationalism and objective reality.

Baudrillard argues that the need to arrive at an objectivized labour loses the reality of other 'archaic' forms of 'labour', notably in the figures of the slave and the artisan. The slave is not just a person plus labour (owned by someone else), but part of a reciprocal relation with the master, who has some level of responsibility for the slave, while the latter is in a position of obligation to the former (pp. 103–4; 94). Here Baudrillard returns to the Hegelian view of the master/slave dialectic literalized and simplified by Marx (see Hegel, *The Phenomenology of Spirit*, pp. 111–19). He is also close to Bataille's take on mastery being itself subject to a pursuit of utility (see Bataille, *The Accursed Share*, vol. III).

The artisan is not simply the possessor of his own labour power, but is part of a society that has the figure of the artisan, who is inseparable from his work and tools. He does not invest, what he puts into the object is lost: 'Death, loss and absence are inscribed in it through the dispossession of the subject, this loss of the subject and the object in the scansion of exchange' (*Mirror*, p. 110; 99). It is the symbolic that is 'irreducibly non-economic' (p. 115; 103) in these relations, and by idealizing the economic labour aspect, there will be no freedom possible other than that offered in capitalist society – the freedom to labour. The primacy of the economic is that which allows and hides other processes of discipline and control. Psychoanalysis is no less complicit with 'the system' than Marxism. The 'Law' of psychoanalysis, based on 'desire', has cancelled reciprocity, offering instead repression and a determinist unconscious. It then exhorts us to overcome the repression, even though it has been *produced* by psychoanalysis.

Baudrillard wishes, nonetheless, to remain radical and offer some possibilities for change. Instead of looking at interior contradictions, we must look to the outside of the code (p. 149; 134). The code here is not a unitary object, but the process of coding that is our rational society's system of signification. Baudrillard argues that blacks question 'race' as code, women and gay liberation question 'sex' as a code (p. 151; 135). It is this coding that must be dealt with, so as to permit actual, constructed 'rights', not the question of specific (and supposedly natural) rights in themselves, which plays the system's game. Baudrillard uses the example of a wealthy immigrant still being seen as an immigrant to demonstrate the primacy of superstructural factors (if we were to insist on this terminology) (p. 155; 136). Rather than attacking the system in a way that is complicit with its functioning, we can transgress the lines, play with the codes. Revolt replaces revolution, as no category can fill the role of revolutionary agent (although there is the suspicion that Baudrillard has such an agent in mind when praising the 'marginal'). The margins threaten the system, although certain specific elements can be recuperated (for example, the (re)selling of 'rebellious' music). Baudrillard cites Foucault on the enclosure of madness, which permitted the functioning of rationality (p. 151; 135). Another possibility is anomie, whether peaceful or leading to apparently gratuitous acts of violence (*Consumer*, pp. 178–80; 286–8). Any radical acts must escape the coding system to re-enter or re-engage the symbolic, which would make (end-oriented) strategies either impossible or redundant depending on the perspective. Baudrillard's notion of utopian revolt centers around the idea that 'utopian violence does not accumulate; it is lost' (*Mirror*, p. 186; 166).

Even at his time of writing, Marx neglected these types of action in favour of the Revolution: Baudrillard cites the *poètes maudits*, machine breakers and sexual revolt as providing examples, from Marx's time, of revolt (p. 178; 159). There are, notes Baudrillard, two versions of Revolution in Marx: pre-1848, it was always possible; post-1848 – the conditions would have to be right. In other words, post-1848, Marx is able to say that if Revolution happens, the conditions were right, and if it does not, then conditions were wrong – a superb tautology. We are forced to wait until we have become aware of the 'reality of the class struggle', as until then, we are divided, alienated in ourselves. Baudrillard argues that anyone is capable of action at any time, as 'each man is totally there at each instant' (p. 186; 166). This peculiar remark can be taken as a strategic device pitched against the Marxist conception of alienation, or it could simply be the *perception* that the 'I' is apparently present as unitary subject. Nonetheless, it seems a simplistic formulation, one that contradicts the systematic anti-humanism of Baudrillard.

Insurrection is still seen by Baudrillard as being potentially radical, as long as it seeks the 'parole' (speech act), thus escaping codification as it is inseparable from the person, who is inseparable within the act. While it does not necessarily entail the physical act of speech, the self-presence of the speech act is clearly valorized here by Baudrillard (symbolic exchange is, at this stage, always some sort of communication, community). If the 'parole' proceeds from the symbolic, in other words *is* symbolic exchange, then where do the materials come from? There are always limits to the form, even if the exchange itself is unlimited (it is impossible to close down in a fixed value (p. 86; 79–80)). The symbolic exchange will never be free from its opponent (value) if we are talking purely of an exchange we call symbolic as prior to the inception of the sign system, and purer. In Baudrillard's terms, there was no such symbolic, it is formulated with its loss. As a result, it will never escape the system that supposedly destroys its (perpetual) originality. In other words, despite appearances, the symbolic does not offer a usable means of escape, and this is not a problem, but an indication of the horizons of any 'outside'. If we alter our perspective such that this 'always lost' aspect takes primacy over the possible revolutionary use value, then we can approach symbolic exchange as being precisely *in* the divide, *in* the relation, a nonplace that is not 'outside' as part of a binary distinction, and therefore capable of disruption. The implicit recommendation in the text of *Mirror* is that the 'mirror of Marxism' be broken, whereby we stop defining our analysis, our possibilities, across the 'power' of Marxism; a power it awarded itself and attempts to universalize. If our critique remains in its terms, we cannot exceed it. Its code must be neglected, voided of its self-proclaimed legitimacy. All critique may be limited by its object, and to 'escape' Marxism to a 'greater' radicality is doubtless just a recasting of the search for legitimacy. To accept the 'creative forgetting' of Marxism here is to recast the early Baudrillard as groping towards a more Bataillean general economy, as opposed to the restricted economies of political economy, Marxism and critique.

Symbolic exchange: from primitivist utopia to reversible death

Baudrillard develops his concept of symbolic exchange from Bataille's notion of 'the accursed share' and of the 'general economy', ideas which in turn come from Mauss's theory of the gift. Baudrillard is by no means uncritical of these sources, but is, I would argue, still reliant on them. Kellner notes that Baudrillard's notion (of symbolic exchange) 'presuppos[es] Bataille's anthropology' (*Baudrillard*, p. 45), although this is not always acknowledged by Baudrillard, and the parallels between the two writers (or the 'influence') extends further than Baudrillard's explicit recognition of it. In fact, even before Marx is more or less discarded, Bataille has taken up residence in Baudrillard's text.

The critique of the 'economic' as such (as it is a fundamental, separable part of our modern era and not of any other historical period) feeds into Baudrillard's take on Bataille's notion of a general economy, which sets Mauss's notion of the gift to work as a principle that is anti-economic, and seeks to be an economy broader than the modern concept of economy. In *The Gift*, Mauss argues that Western ideas of exchange are limited, and that 'it is only our Western societies that quite recently turned man into an "economic animal"' (*The Gift*, p. 74). We have forgotten gift-economies, as exemplified in the potlatch. This is an adversarial form of gift-giving where to give creates an obligation to receive and also to return the gift. This returned gift must be bigger and better than the first, and can even extend to the destruction of your own offering. There can be no equivalent to modern property in such a system, and all exchange takes place in the context of religious, political, ritual, social interaction, as none of these has yet acquired an autonomous existence.

Bataille extends this theory to sacrifice, arguing that the fundamental principle of the universe consists of waste, destruction, death, eroticism and transgression, rather than truth, wealth, security. There must always be an 'accursed share' to keep the system going. Bataille believes that we ought to behave in ways that encourage this 'general economy' of expenditure over the limited or 'restricted' economy of economics, but that this is almost impossible to realize: it is a paradoxical utopianism, which is also how we should see symbolic exchange.

Early on, Baudrillard is interested in this expenditure (*dépense*) as it is opposed to the rationale behind (capitalist) economy, which is accumulative and conservational, and spending is seen as a function of growth. Baudrillard notes the Bataillean version of consumption/consummation ('la consumation', *Consumer*, p. 157; 249–50), whereby objects are consumed in sacrificial gift and/or destruction (i.e. forms of Maussian potlatch). Baudrillard opposes this to the view of the contemporary 'time consumption' which is either time spent labouring or allocated 'leisure time', productively used (*Consumer*, p. 158; 250). Consummation entails the using up of the object, rather than using it usefully, as use (value), which consumer society, as an extension of capitalism, insists on. The productionist argument, whereby societies are defined by their mode of production, would have it that the sacrifice comes from objects that are surplus to a subsistence level. In *For a Critique*, utility and use value are at stake, and the order of precedence between sacrifice/destruction and accumulation is reversed. Baudrillard refers to Bataille with regard to 'value' in destruction, initially on the subject of leisure time and the exhortation to make use of it (p. 77; 79). Following Bataille, however, a more genuine 'value' can be gained in wasting this time, instead of extracting value from it (for example, not going on holiday). The notion of value, as it appears here, is awkward in both Bataille and Baudrillard, as there is a presumption of a 'meta-value', of a real worth that is beyond the fixed values of the sign and economic systems. A generous reading would concede that this new value is unmeasurable. Alternatively, it could be argued that they have returned to what is merely a different order of the value both try so hard to escape.

As a further illustration of how value is now something to be destroyed, Baudrillard makes a further reference to Bataille, when discussing the purchase of works of art. At an auction, in particular, the value, if there is one, is in the sumptuary expenditure – and not because the painting, for example, is actually worth the amount spent on it, or even that the painting is worth having in terms of artistic value (*For a Critique*, p. 117; 135). This is due to the collapse of the economic value of the money involved in this transaction (how is the value to be determined? How can it be made or kept commensurate with its object – the purchased painting?), and the loss of the symbolic effect of the painting (as the space of communication between artist and viewer) as it becomes mediated by economic exchange. Although the destruction of value somehow eludes the 'System' of values we are caught in, only the system itself can now undo itself. Note also, that Baudrillard moves beyond the critique of market (exchange) value over a supposed real value. The artwork has no real value here, and money itself loses value when in contact with art, so the commodity itself as a form is doubly undone.

As Baudrillard develops his critique of Marx, Bataille's often implicit importance increases. Bataille is the key to resisting fixed economies of signs or of capital: 'sacrificial economy for Bataille, or symbolic exchange, are excluded from political economy and its critique, which is only its realised form' (*For a Critique*, p. 43 trans. mod.; 42). Baudrillard's non-critique of the wilful universalization of Mauss that is Bataille's 'accursed share' shows his fundamental acceptance of Bataillean anti-economics. He maintains that Bataille has ' "naturalized" Mauss, but in a metaphysical spiral so prodigious that the reproach is not really one' ('When Bataille attacked', p. 61; 5), thereby approving of his *approach* at least as much as of the theory itself. This approach also signals Baudrillard's interest in the radical possibilities of 'challenge' (*le défi*) that are essential to symbolic exchange as a theory.[22]

Baudrillard's conception of the symbolic forms gradually, and not always clearly, in the course of *For a Critique*. This new emphasis, away from sign systems, leads to symbolic exchange, which for Baudrillard, is the *only* form of the symbolic. Throughout this book, symbolic exchange is that which is excluded from the relations of signifier/signified and use value/exchange value. It is what is excluded from value, as it is ambivalence (pp. 98–101; 109–12). At this stage, the concept is hardly developed further by Baudrillard, but operates as a highly tautological device, to represent something which has been lost in the functioning and totalization of the sign system (pp. 98, 109; 160–1, 196). For the most part, at this stage, Baudrillard refers to the symbolic, only developing this into symbolic exchange near the end (pp. 207–9; 261–3). For Baudrillard, as I have noted earlier, this symbolic 'is not (a) value.

It is loss, (re)solution of value and the positivity of the sign' (p. 161 trans. mod.; 196). This statement is possibly the most crucial 'formulation' of symbolic exchange in its function as a form of 'différance'. It is always beyond, and constitutes a privileged, if always already constituted, Other. Baudrillard specifically differentiates his conception from the Lacanian Symbolic. Whereas the latter appears as the installation of the Law, for Baudrillard, it is the Law and repression that destroy the symbolic (*For a Critique*, pp. 161–2; 196–8, also *Mirror*, p. 61; 65). The symbolic cannot simply be repressed, as this too would mean recuperation as value, even if only 'negatively', as the repressed.

Where the symbolic came from is never made clear by Baudrillard, and in some senses it ends in replacing the referent Baudrillard has tried so hard to displace in *For a Critique*, as the actual real, as opposed to reality as referent.[23] It is this latter form of the real that has displaced the symbolic, the real is 'never anything other than the simulacrum of the symbolic' (*For a Critique*, p. 162; 198). The real is seen by Baudrillard as being a sanitized, controlled re-creation of the symbolic, which essentially seems to mean the stage at which discrete value (binary oppositions with presence/absence at the base) has no hold.

In symbolic exchange the subject is at stake (*For a Critique*, p. 208; 263), and the object becomes nothing (p. 212; 267), such that the object is annulled and the subjects are no longer discrete, but *joined* in the difference, not separated by it. Baudrillard certainly appears to believe that culture did live in this symbolic (with its rituals constituting symbolic exchange) only being forcibly ejected with the institution of total signification, which could be seen as being at the start of language, or as Baudrillard seems to imply, when capitalism and signification colluded in valuing everything.

In *Mirror*, Baudrillard continues to develop the symbolic, but the precise nature of it remains unclear. Increasingly, it becomes apparent that this uncertainty is due to the nature of symbolic exchange, which, as ambivalence, and disruption of value(s), cannot be precisely defined and retain its force. However, Baudrillard does attribute an approximate originality to symbolic exchange 'symbolic circulation is primordial' (p. 79; 86), and that to remain revolutionary, we ought to pursue this symbolic relation.[24]

Once again, Baudrillard emphasizes that 'the symbolic must never be confused with the psychological' (p. 102; 114), as it is 'irreducibly non-economic' (p. 103; 115); that is, it cannot be retained within a system of values, and, in addition, individuals are not autonomous producers/products except within a system where production is dominant (modern Western society). Within such a system, however, the symbolic dimension can re-appear through acts of revolt and rejection of imposed coding of groups, for example, women, blacks (*Mirror*, p. 139; 156). Baudrillard sees this type of action as being on the increase (writing in the wake of 1968), as increasing categorization and standardization have induced a demand for the lost symbolic. It is perhaps necessary to restate that Baudrillard is not being as wildly or simplistically utopian as he may appear at this stage. There is no suggestion of a process of an increase in 'symbolic' acts of violence (in terms of spectacle, for example) which will usher in a benevolent, unified society where symbolic exchange is the norm, as '[this] utopian violence does not accumulate; it is lost' (p. 166; 186). It is sacrificial, not beneficial. Nonetheless, there is still a sense of possibility, and, somewhat perversely, given the effort Baudrillard makes to empty out organized political revolt, this can take the form of political action, as long as this is not limited to traditionally privileged groupings such as the working class.

This semi-transcendental, not ambiguous enough, form of the symbolic – as a possible, more authentic real – is largely removed in *Symbolic Exchange*, where symbolic exchange becomes a finally irretrievable, fleeting instance. Symbolic exchange remains momentary, yet always repeats the originary moment of its exclusion. The breakdown of presence/absence, subject/object, and so on, revolves around death, the rejection of which is seen as having installed the code (signification). So far in Baudrillard, symbolic exchange has remained largely unformulated, lurking as an idealized Other away from capitalism and its Marxist critique, but with *Symbolic Exchange*, the development of the counter-gift that follows on from Bataille's recasting of the gift initiates a more coherent (but still diffuse) theorization. In the first place, the Sun is proposed as source of life and exemplar of the gift: 'solar energy is the source of life's exuberant development. The origin and essence of our wealth are given in the radiation of the Sun, which dispenses energy (wealth) without any return. The Sun gives without ever receiving' (Bataille, *The Accursed Share*, p. 28). Second, the individual is called on to acknowledge the primacy of the gift:

> We need on the one hand to go beyond the narrow limits within which we ordinarily remain, and on the other hand somehow bring our going-beyond back within our limits . . . Gift-giving has the virtue of a surpassing of the subject who gives, but in exchange for the object given, the subject appropriates the surpassing. (*The Accursed Share*, p. 69)

It is not all so suggestive of transcendence, with our mucky origins also to the fore: 'life is a product of putrefaction' (*The Accursed Share*, vol. II, p. 63), which we increasingly try to ignore. Waste is a crucial part of Bataille's version of gift-giving: it is not benevolence that drives the Sun, but waste, and the necessity of waste. Sacrifice, for Bataille, brings gift-giving and waste together in a human response to this 'general economy' based on expenditure. The fully formulated version of symbolic exchange extends Bataille's general economy and estranges his own symbolic from the somewhat easy answers provided in *For a Critique* and *Mirror*, given that the symbolic was supposed to be opposed to all values, all ordinarily produced reals within capitalism. Here, according to Kellner, 'non-reproductive, "pulsating" sex, exhibitionism, non-utilitarian waste and gratuitous violence serve as paradigms of "symbolic exchange"' (Kellner, *Baudrillard*, p. 45).

Baudrillard imputes the process of symbolic exchange to the workings of the general economy. The counter-gift (from the process of outbidding in the potlatch form) is 'the single truly symbolic process, which in fact implies death as a kind of maximal excess' ('When Bataille attacked', p. 61 trans. mod.; 5).[25] As stated earlier, Baudrillard is wary of the naturalization of the gift (hence his drawing out of the counter-gift as prevailing principle), yet he barely differs from Bataille's use of the notion of the gift. Baudrillard develops the counter-gift through reversibility (*Symbolic Exchange*, p. 2; 8), the defining, organizing (non) centre of which is death.

The new excess of capital

Capital's success has removed it from the real, and as a result 'the real has died' (*Symbolic Exchange*, p. 7; 19). Capitalism has long been dominant, according to Baudrillard, in its manner of spreading value (as fixed attribute and/or attributability) (p. 10; 23), but finally succeeds in bringing about the 'structural form of value' (p. 8; 20) which is where values exchange against each other rather than against a testable real. Thus, the apotheosis of Value – its full totalization – is its disappearance as a genuine category.[26] The freeing of capital is linked with the increase in 'dead labour', in the form of machines, which also free labour (and constitute the final death of labour).

Labour is now not the opponent of capital but enmeshed with it (p. 35; 61). Salary can no longer be seen to represent labour plus surplus value (as capitalists view it) or surplus value including a labour cost (as Marx identifies it). Instead salary is now a 'sacrament', that grants you your citizenship (and allows consumption) (p. 19; 37). Labour now only signifies itself (p. 11; 25), and 'non-productive work' is also brought into the system (such as Welfare State payments). The 'economy' and 'growth' are now the 'aims of capital', and 'good' for society, while labour is an end in itself. Therefore, argues Baudrillard, the classical political economy (including the Marxist version) no longer subsists. Kellner argues that to an extent this may hold true, but that Baudrillard's assertion of the end of material(ist) primacy is an example of his 'sign fetishism' (*Baudrillard*, p. 107), which ignores real, material relations and (inevitably) domination by capital. The critique could of course be reversed: what about Marx's 'material fetishism'? To an extent, Baudrillard would presumably not dispute the dominance of capital, but, for him, this 'dominance' is in a form that differs widely from Kellner's view. Baudrillard argues that capitalism is no longer the possession of 'capitalists', and that capital is itself a term that becomes highly unstable in a world of notional money and where the increase in technologization means that the workforce is not doubly oppressed, but is increasingly pointless, whether in terms of a 'maintenance' of capital or a 'revolution of the proletariat' (this last point is what distinguishes Baudrillard from Ernest Mandel's 'late capitalism').

The problematic, for Baudrillard, is of a different nature. This initially results from the situation of labour and capital. Work is now a gift on the part of the capitalist: 'In fact, it appears that the worker donates capital to the employer and in return the capitalist provides work to the worker: it is in the power of the capitalist to initiate the gift' (Gane, *Bestiary*, pp. 89–90). This is turned back by Baudrillard to the initial functioning of capital, which, in separating out values to represent a real, and in creating a functional workforce, attempts, and largely succeeds, in giving an irreversible gift, such that 'the system lives on symbolic violence' (*Symbolic Exchange*, p. 36; 62). Here, symbolic violence is seen as that which breaks apart the symbolic exchange of gift/counter-gift, where 'challenge, reversal and overbidding are the law' (p. 36; 63). Symbolic violence is the attempt to prevent symbolic exchange, and is the attempt at the unilateral gift – which is the unanswerable imposition of an unchangeable, unavoidable system – following which, revolts, dissent and demands about pay or conditions become assimilable if they follow the logic of this attempt. Marxist revolutionary rhetoric, for example, limits the possible change to be gained within the categories of production/capital that it purports to oppose. Symbolic violence is what initiates the code, system, etc., and remains a resource for these. Baudrillard insists on the counter-gift, as the only possible revolt. This is the attempted returning of an unanswerable gift (work, which leads to the slow death of workers), a gift which can only be thwarted by the actually unanswerable gift of death itself. The threat of death or suicide then threatens the unilateral 'generosity' of production in accumulation.[27] This too would be symbolic violence. It does not attack the system, but recalls the process which initiated it, and therefore also the possibility of its non-being. In a subtle recasting of Mauss and Bataille, Baudrillard also warns that 'the gift' is our myth, the Other for value, whereas symbolic exchange functions as counter-gift (already-implied reversibility):

> The gift is *our* myth, the idealist myth correlative to our materialist myth, and we bury the primitives under both myths at the same time. The primitive symbolic process knows nothing of the gratuity of the gift, it knows only the challenge and the reversibility of exchanges . . .

The primitives know . . . *that nothing is without return,* not in a contractual sense, but in the sense that the process of exchange is inevitably reversible. (pp. 48–9n trans. mod.; 63n)

Those societies that have symbolic exchange are *in* it, rather than in the business of exchanging objects so as to be more highly defined subject-givers (as Derrida maintains, after Heidegger, in *Given Time I*). Baudrillard argues that it is only we (in the capitalist West) who seek the dual valuing of economic exchange and gift as parallel exchanges of controllable objects, and that 'primitive' societies are not in either form of exchange that we 'recognize'. Symbolic violence does not stop gifts altogether, but sets them up as exceptions, defining when they occur, and removing most of the 'gift-economy' in the process.

The attempt at the irreversible gift can only be opposed, according to Baudrillard, not by being the 'opposite' of the system, but by the radical alterity it seeks to exclude. So, for example, the working class is opposed to the owners of the (capitalist) means of production, but this limits their chances of meaningfully opposing the system. Organizing as a class, excluding the 'lumpenproletariat', merely does the work of capital. Baudrillard gives the following examples of actions approaching symbolic exchange: an arbitrary strike which does not have as its aim the winning of a fixed gain from the capitalist or the taking of hostages, which largely insists on incommensurable exchange, even to the point of not demanding anything other than recognition of the challenge itself. Ultimately, Baudrillard suggests, the challenge (*défi*) or counter-gift must take the form of death, as only in the sacrifice of death can the slowly administered death that is labour be disrupted or annulled, as 'a man must die to become labour power' (*Symbolic Exchange*, p. 39; 67). This appears to mean real (biological) death for the contesting party – and it brings death to the system in a punctual/punctuating way – as death is no longer to be seen as that which is conquered and outside the system: it has invaded once more. Death, then, can bring the reversibility or rupture to the totalized capital/value system.[28] This is because it has been *systematically* excluded in order to found the unitary logic that is the attribution of value and binary opposition. Death is the founding

discrimination that closed off symbolic exchange, where it constituted reversibility as a positive element (p. 126; 195), 'and the
absence of death alone permits of our exchange of values and the
play of equivalences' (p. 154; 236). For Baudrillard, it is essentially
capital that has closed off the symbolic, and attempts to combat the
political economy of capitalism reveal that now lost dimension as
a possible alternative (even if this alternative is unattainable).
Baudrillard leaves the world of capital behind to look at societies
that were or are in symbolic exchange, and that include, rather
than exclude death. Initiation takes the form of symbolic death,
acceptance of and into the realm of the dead, who are still among
the living, such that:

> they pass . . . to a death that is *given* and *received*, and that is therefore
> reversible in social exchange, 'soluble' in exchange. At the same time
> the opposition between birth and death disappears: they can also be
> *exchanged* under the form of symbolic reversibility. (p. 132; 203)

The term symbolic death conveys the dual (multiple) nature that
death takes outside of the Value system. At one level, symbolic
death shows a use of 'symbolic' that Baudrillard has largely surpassed, where a certain event stands in for another. But
Baudrillard's symbolic is (somewhat tautologically) that which is
imbued; therefore, in addition to a 'pretend' death, what we regard
as real death is also in play, as it is not, according to Baudrillard,
split off in the same way that modern Western culture, in particular, splits death from life. The initiate enacts both of the above
aspects, and equally stands for the reversibility of death: on the one
hand, he has been with the dead, and is now back; on the other, this
means that the dead are accessible, and have a vital role in initiating the start of (adult) life. Baudrillard pinpoints our removal from
the symbolic to the promise of immortality, leading to the exclusion
of death, and the need to accumulate and defer, in this life (p. 129;
199), such that we also gain in the next life. As we do not exchange
with death, it becomes that which haunts us – an extreme version
of which is Freud's 'death drive', which Baudrillard sees as
approaching the problem of death's exclusion, although Freud does
not go as far as Bataille, and Baudrillard argues that the theory of
the 'death drive' still means we experience death as excluded. The

death drive is the (perhaps ultimate) expression of 'a rationalization of death' such that 'the death drive is at the same time the system, and the system's *double*' (p. 152; 203). It is Bataille that Baudrillard sees as having come closest to expressing the role of death away from a rationalist logic of exclusion. Baudrillard is being disingenuous to only mention Bataille overtly at this point, as he is already operating within the notion of general economy. For Bataille, we are always defined by our resistance to death, nature, decay and loss of self, but it is in some way our duty to approach, rather than reject them outright. If we do, as modern rational society does, then 'death exists in it [the real world] in a contained state, but fills it up' (Bataille, *The Accursed Share*, vol. III, p. 220).

According to Baudrillard, for Bataille, 'death is excess, ambivalence, gift, sacrifice and paroxysm' (*Symbolic Exchange*, p. 154 trans. mod.; 237) that is in no way separable from the 'participants' in, for example, eroticism. Death is another expression of the loss of subject and object in 'intimacy'. For Bataille, death is some sort of 'beyond', but it is the beyond that is prior to that which we experience as (present) being. The West has death as that which is excluded, and consciousness based on this exclusion (as exemplified in Hegel or Heidegger, for example). The subject issues from the exclusion of death and the myth that 'explains' it (*Symbolic Exchange*, p. 159; 244). With the emphasis on biological death and the 'Other', the body is the site of death, and can thus be marked off from the soul. Biological death only appears (historically and conceptually) after symbolic death. Our only myth is that of science: 'biology is pregnant with death, and the body taking shape within it is pregnant with death' (p. 166; 253). The ensuing separation means that the 'I' of the subject lives in 'the biological simulacrum of our own body' (p. 166; 254). All societies have 'staved off the abjection of natural death, with the *social* abjection of decomposition' (p. 179 trans. mod.; 274), yet 'primitive' societies 'concede[s] the dead their difference (p. 181; 275). In other words, the 'actuality' of death is both a difference in itself, and a difference that can be internal to symbolic exchange, unlike in our modern society where death is sanitized, controlled or denied, and even frozen, as an event that has not yet really happened (cryogenics).

Natural death, then, is a Western concept that accompanies the separation of Nature as a non-privileged site. Societies of symbolic exchange have been able to inscribe the loss, waste and absence among the movements of symbolic exchange, which occur at the 'real' level of familiarity and involvement with death, at the 'representational' level of language, ritual formulae, and as the effect both have on the society as a whole. All of these elements together mean symbolic exchange is occurring, and slipping between real and unreal, true and false, self and other, all 'mediated' by death:

> the symbolic is neither a concept, an agency, a category, nor a 'structure', but an act of exchange and a *social relation which puts an end to the real*, which resolves the real, and at the same time, puts an end to the opposition between the real and the imaginary. (p. 133; 204)

So, symbolic exchange is this non-place of the play of difference and ambiguity, but I believe Baudrillard has moved on from having this as a privileged 'Outside', to a position where the ontological question of Being as presence (as) opposed to absence is being posed. The apparently opposed (or separate) problematic of simulation also raises this question, 'from the other side' (or inside), challenging concepts of the real on the grounds of their excessive realism.

Notes

1. An example of metafunctionality is the gadget, as it is overly specialized to the point of being less useful than the object it claims to supersede. Non-functional objects are objects that for example, take their value as part of a collection.
2. See *For a Critique*, pp. 143–64; 172–99.
3. See, for example, the discussions of credit (*System*, pp. 156–63; 218–26); or the effects of the system of production on technique (pp. 47, 123–5; 68, 175–6 among others); or the section on the 'socio-ideological system of objects and consumption' (pp. 135–55; 189–217).
4. A conception which itself provides the object of critique in *Mirror*.
5. This is most apparent in *Mirror*, which viciously and continuously attacks 'Freudo-marxism'. Baudrillard's distaste for such

formulations can safely be presumed to apply just as much to *System* as to any other writer.

6. Which will itself be problematized in *For a Critique*.

7. In a further footnote, Freud adds that the 'foot represents a woman's penis, the absence of which is deeply felt' (*The Essentials of Psychoanalysis*, p. 299n) by the viewer. The key to phallocentric psychoanalysis is this absence that constitutes the female and allows the male subject to *be*.

8. For a reading of sadomasochism and fetishism that escapes the presuppositions and the presumption of pathology, see Deleuze, *Coldness and Cruelty*, in *Masochism*, pp. 9–138. This text could also serve as a 'demystification' of Marxoid pathologization of the object, as objectness is re-assessed in what we may wish to call a general economy, as opposed to the restricted economy of fixed values and 'bad objects'.

9. Baudrillard presents us with a highly idealized subject that somehow existed before the problem of the unified Subject arose, i.e. the society of rationality. Perhaps it is the reconstitution that constitutes the Subject as a category. He does mention this, only to posit a potential 'real', pre-existing subject.

10. This emphasis on illusion declines as Baudrillard progresses to his theorization of simulation. It returns in mutated form as 'radical illusion' in later texts. This is an originary illusion, which can be seen, in hindsight, as granting the possibility of truth, as with Nietzsche's assertion that 'nothing is true, everything is permitted', where the impossibility of Truth is the condition for any truth to occur. Baudrillard's theory of simulation begins to emerge in *Consumer*, notably in the section 'Beyond True and False' (pp. 126–8; 196–9).

11. Baudrillard may be accused of universalizing here himself, but these excesses and poverties only become structural – that is, fixed – with the arrival of economic exchange and its precedence over other forms of exchange.

12. See also 'Requiem for the Media', in *For a Critique*, pp. 164–84; 200–18, and p. 175; 216 in particular.

13. Charles Levin, 'Introduction', in *For a Critique*, pp. 5–28.

14. This ostensibly refers, in the text, to nudity being part of the

system of clothing rather than as some symbolic act, but it is generalizable for all (objects of) fetishism (for Baudrillard).

15. Baudrillard exempts the Barthes of *S/Z*, and Derrida from this generalization.

16. This line should appear on page 161 in the English edition, but it is not there.

17. This term can be translated as pleasure or orgasm, but has come to imply something greater than those, something not determined by a goal or end, while still connected to desire (see, for example, Barthes, *The Pleasure of the Text*).

18. Baudrillard's symbolic is beyond that of Lacan, whom he accuses of still maintaining an ideal, repressed content (*For a Critique*, p. 161; 197). If anything, Baudrillard's symbolic is directly opposed to Lacan's (conception of the) Symbolic, as this latter form is the arrival of the Law, i.e. of (fixed) value, and Baudrillard's symbolic could more accurately be read as a parallel of Julia Kristeva's notion of the semiotic.

19. 'The worker becomes a revolutionary not by being more of a worker, but by losing his workerness' (Murray Bookchin, *Post-Scarcity Anarchism*, p. 188).

20. The English text has 'speculative dead end' for 'specularité indépassable' (*Le Miroir de la production*, p. 29), which misses the point.

21. Baudrillard's specific example here is the Marxist anthropologist Godelier.

22. Both writers have been criticized for their 'primitivism', Jean-François Lyotard among the critics (Pefanis, *Heterology*, p. 134). Baudrillard, however, is not arguing that so-called primitive societies have something better than Western society through their primitiveness, but that this symbolic exchange is not primitive (in terms of being previous, inferior or 'savage'). Genosko points out Lyotard's argment is compromised by his belief in desire as a fundamental category, and that he is 'at least as nostalgic for a hippie anti-economy as Baudrillard' (*Baudrillard and Signs*, p. 90).

23. At this stage in the Baudrillard œuvre, *le réel* has not yet come to be used as being the operation of a notional, 'consensual' real, as opposed to a genuine reality. Here, *le réel*/the real

stands for the actual existing world, insofar as this is given credence by Baudrillard.

24. Even if Baudrillard is plainly not following a Marxist approach, he does see himself as continuing the revolutionary aspect that Marx himself left incomplete (*Mirror*, p. 51; 51).

25. It is worth noting that for both Bataille and Baudrillard, death has a fluid character, sliding from being biological, to transcendental, to ideological, etc. They both oppose the fixing of death as the Outside (although this is, of necessity, implied) which they see as having been exacerbated in modern Western culture, even if the process started earlier.

26. As Pefanis notes, for Baudrillard, 'when something is everywhere, it is nowhere' (*Heterology*, p. 71).

27. A generosity based on theft, Marx would argue. Baudrillard's choice of 'gift' here is particularly irksome to Marxists, given that Marx is acerbic about the generosity and 'abstemiousness' of capital and capitalists. Marx writes of the capitalist class heroically not consuming its wealth, and risking it in the means of production, which are actually what produce its wealth, through the extraction of surplus value from those lucky enough to be 'given' work (*Capital*, vol. I, p. 745).

28. Written in the mid-1970s, this nonetheless applies strongly to much more recent acts of devastating force at many 'symbolic' levels, such as the attack on the World Trade Center (see Chapter 4 for Baudrillard's controversial reading of this event).

Chapter 2

Simulation and the Decay of the Real

Orders of simulacra, phases of the image

Even though 'the real' relegates and seeks to destroy symbolic exchange, it always already contains the seeds of its own destruction, as for Baudrillard, there has never been any unmediated reality. Although a world of symbolic exchange would seem to be more real, any realness is caught up in ambiguity, death, sacrifice, violence. Furthermore, just like the ordinary real, it is never present, *here*. It has always gone missing. So, instead of a true reality, we get various types of simulacra, which present themselves as real. The more simulation becomes complete, the more we have a sense of the real, of being immersed in reality. So the real is a middle term between symbolic exchange and simulation, but it is also the product of simulacra, and nothing more.

Baudrillard's first analysis of simulation, which he comes to see as the dominant mode of perception or 'experience' of the world, is in *Symbolic Exchange*. Baudrillard sketches a genealogy which mirrors Foucault's notion of *épistémès*, as set out in *The Order of Things*. In feudal society, there are 'natural' signs which remain in their set position, in parallel with the social structure. As we leave this system, the sign becomes freer, and competition stimulates the counterfeit, the possibility of pretence through imitation (the first order of simulacra). This still imputes a realness to the sign, in that the counterfeit can be a realistic copy (therefore partaking of and enhancing the idea of the natural sign). Baudrillard uses stucco as the exemplary form, as it covers, and imitates nature via form. This process of copying precedes possible production of the real

(*Symbolic Exchange*, p. 51; 79–80). This next stage, the second order of simulacra, takes the form of production and reiterates his earlier writings on the sign, such that this second stage is the era of the 'political economy of the sign', the era of representation of a real. It is the industrial era, or, approximately, modernity.

These earlier stages are really only a pretext for Baudrillard to propose that the order of simulacra we now inhabit (the third) is simulation, and here there is no real to imitate (again we can refer back to the vanishing referent in previous texts) as the simulation is not an imitation, but a replacement. This phase is one of the 'structural law of value' (p. 50; 77), where the code reigns. This is not a code that is a specific, hidden value system, but the principle of the code: all can stem from models, rather than appearing naturally, then get 'coded'. Before moving on to a survey of Baudrillard's notion that we currently inhabit 'simulation', it is worth looking at his other formulation of the 'genealogy' of simulacra, now seen to occur in four phases. This will help us broach the question of how our supposed current situation differs from preceding modes of viewing reality:

> Whereas representation attempts to absorb simulation by interpreting it as a false representation, simulation envelops the whole edifice of representation as itself a simulacrum.
>
> Such would be the successive phases of the image:
> – it is the reflection of a profound reality
> – it masks and perverts a profound reality
> – it masks the *absence* of a profound reality
> – it bears no relation to any reality whatever: it is its own pure simulacrum.
>
> (*Simulacra and Simulation*, p. 6; 16–17)

Overall, it seems that there is a move to an increased emphasis on the 'real' as it slips away. This occurs at the cultural level, and is mirrored in Baudrillard's texts; the irony being that the writer most hostile to reality is the one who uses (requires) it most (Levin calls Baudrillard a 'perverse Platonist' (*Jean Baudrillard*, p. 82), for, as he sees it, echoing Plato's critique of imitation). For Baudrillard, these different orders or phases are entwined levels of simulation rather than a succession, and would seem to follow on from the (retrospective) lack of symbolic exchange that drives our culture to real-ize, i.e. all of the above phases are 'strategies of the real', our attempts to constrain ambiguity. Although not explicitly stated, our culture has not *known* (could it have?) a real free of any system of simulacra. Baudrillard's use of phases of the *image* suggests that we are not dealing with a knowable reality lost in the schemings of bad representation (i.e. reality hidden by ideology) as all that we have ever looked at was already an *image*, not the real world via an image, and that at a certain point (the first phase), the simulacra were seen to coincide with their reality, the essence of something and its appearance being inseparable. Does Baudrillard intend this reading? If so, it makes our 'era of simulation' not too dissimilar from this starting point.[1] I would contend that while this may not be Baudrillard's intention, this can be read through the text. So his intent may well be that 'the reflection of a basic reality' is just that – a faithful display of a genuine reality.[2] Even if this were the case, Baudrillard's model for 'genuine reality', beyond constructed reality, is symbolic exchange, which cannot be represented, or *reflected* in the image that is the necessary moment of real-ization (symbolic exchange is to a certain extent outside of the construction of the real, and in general, it is symbolic exchange, if anything, that haunts simulation as a term free from mediation). There are always images, and the image removes the reality of whatever may or may not be there. For Baudrillard, we can never break through to an unmediated reality, as there are only ways of looking at reality, which constitute its realness. His texts on simulation do not have a genuine reality as a necessary base, they deal instead with alterations in the perception of reality, and this perception is as much real as there is.

The second phase is equivalent to the counterfeit, the third to production, and the fourth is Baudrillard's main concern (simulation). The four phases, like the three orders of simulacra, signal that there is an element of progress towards the final stage. The fourth phase of the image is equivalent to the third order of simulacra, but the use made of phases insists less on assigning a set, historically determined place for each element of development. The phases of the image also install 'basic reality' as a category that is always within simulatedness.

Nonetheless, there is a suggestion of progression, and that our supposed occupation of the third order of simulation, where simulation no longer copies anything, is seen by Baudrillard as definitively different from preceding modes of perception, as this one is supposed by him to supersede all others, as it removes the possibility of representation. Baudrillard characterizes this contemporary era as being one of nostalgia, as we carry on trying to represent, to make sense, when there is no real to be found, but to some extent, it is the absence of recognition of his own nostalgia that in a sense allows Baudrillard to use the term, both explicitly and implicitly as a criticism. He is therefore insinuated in what he criticizes, although not in such a way that would fatally compromise the theorization of simulation. Nietzsche has pursued a similar argumentation, collapsing the 'true' and 'apparent' worlds in *The Twilight of the Idols*. For Nietzsche, the perception of access to the real world follows a similar pattern to Baudrillard's schema, and the later stages can serve as clarification for the appearance of simulation:

> 4. The true world – is it unattainable? At all events it is unattained. And as unattained it is also *unknown*. Consequently it no longer comforts, nor saves, nor constrains: what could something unknown constrain us to? . . .
> 5. The 'true world' – an idea that no longer serves any purpose, that no longer constrains one to anything, – a useless idea that has become quite superfluous, consequently an exploded idea: let us abolish it! . . .
> 6. We have suppressed the true world: what world survives? the apparent world perhaps? . . . Certainly not! *In abolishing the true world we have also abolished the world of appearance!* (p. 25)

What Nietzsche describes parallels Baudrillard's account of simulation, as Nietzsche's true world is seen to become a 'true world', at a given time, but has to be read back as the precondition for the attempts to say otherwise, i.e. only once we have a 'true' world, can we claim there is or was a genuinely true world. Representation cannot function by itself, so we cannot talk of a fundamental, qualitative difference between the real and representation. If at any stage such a point is reached, then the realness of the real at all other points has to be called into question.

Baudrillard's essay 'The Precession of Simulacra' (*Simulacra and*

Simulation), which hones the move to simulation seen in *Symbolic Exchange*, has nostalgia as a dominant figure, continually stressing the disappearance of various stages of the real. The tension of nostalgia permeates the essay, and is exemplified in the following: 'when the real is no longer what it used to be, nostalgia assumes its full meaning. There is a plethora of myths of origin and of signs of reality' (*Simulacra and Simulation*, p. 6 trans. mod.; 17). Although the reference to the real is certainly playful, with the connotation of being 'past it' or no longer being up to the job, this reference exemplifies the text as a whole: by continuous reference to something 'no longer' there, this missing real is given more retrospective substance in its absence. Equally, the proliferation noted by Baudrillard appears in his own text, deviated into a proliferation of signs of falsity and suggestive absence. It is perhaps worthwhile to open out just what Baudrillard means by nostalgia. In general terms, he goes on to say that:

> [There is] a plethora of second-hand truth, objectivity and authenticity. There is an escalation of the true, of lived experience; resurrection of the figurative where the object and substance have disappeared. Panic-stricken production of the real, above and parallel to the panic of material production. (p. 7 trans. mod.; 17)

Baudrillard writes a kind of litany of what is gone, which I feel shows some of the problems that Baudrillard gives himself, ending as he does with something approaching a Hegelian view of History, even if this History never had a *real* existence: 'No more subject, focal point, center or periphery . . . no more violence or surveillance' (p. 29 trans. mod.; 51). Baudrillard then goes on to declare the end of panoptic (and representational) space, and that therefore, 'there is no longer any medium in the literal sense' (p. 30; 53). Even if we allow that Baudrillard is not saying that these things had a genuinely real existence, but that they are elements of a system where the real is produced (possibly as power-effect), we are still left with the sense that an epoch is past, and the world has passed into a new phase. In the wake of this lies the substance that Baudrillard is forced to grant these aspects of a real now supposedly extinct. The absence that Baudrillard confers on them (are they perhaps only identifiable as/when absent?) means that the 'era of the real' lingers as a necessary backdrop for Baudrillard to be able to assert that anything has changed. If he specifies that simulation is transhistorical, then without some kind of analysis of the 'ontology' of simulation, simulation *is*, and there is therefore no qualitative change when the 'third order of simulacra' takes over. If simulation is purely at a social/historical level (i.e. the level of the real), then Baudrillard has too simplistic and problematic a version of history to allow the theory of simulation to work. The historical aspect is insufficient as it does not say why we should suddenly, even if not instantly, lose representation as a link to the real.

It is also clear that simulation is not just simply something we submit to, as on occasion, Baudrillard valorizes simulation as a strategy against the tyranny of the real, advocating at one point a simulated hold-up as challenge (as it can only be punished as a real act, not as a simulation) (*Simulacra and Simulation*, pp. 19–21; 36–9). Hoax bomb calls are punished as crimes, and that is correct if the call aimed to really suggest there was a bomb placed somewhere. But if the call was a simulation, the system is shown not to be able to distinguish between 'real' and simulation. The advocacy of 'hypersimulation' only makes sense if simulation is at least partially transhistorical, as it implies that simulation is not just an effect of the era of (re)production, for example (this also implies that Baudrillard's critique of the limiting capacity of the 'political economy of the sign' would be much reduced, as the sign becomes just one version of simulation, rather than the definitive attack on symbolic exchange).

The appearance of simulation

For Baudrillard, it is the success of capital/value/production/the real that leads to its demise through saturation. Even the most material of productive constructs loses its specificity. For example, the factory 'disappears', as it becomes one of the models of society, and 'society as a whole takes on the appearance of the factory' (*Symbolic Exchange*, p. 18; 35). The transformation of the real (as produced) into the hyperreal centres on the changing role of money with regard to traditional capital (resources for profit through expansion). The growth of production that necessitated increased dealing in money is seen by Baudrillard as inducing a removal of *significance* from production itself. This is dated by Baudrillard to the Crash of 1929 (*Symbolic Exchange*, p. 21; 39) and the collapse of many currencies in the 1920s and 1930s, but it is perhaps more useful to take this event as a recognition of an already complete process. Baudrillard also cites the loss of the gold standard as the loss of any possible reference (and draws a parallel with the loss of the unified subject in favour of the unconscious) (p. 23; 42). This leads to the installation of the 'economic' as the rationale for production, and the economic needs only 'the mythical operation of the economy' (p. 33; 59) for its reproduction: it is seen as important that the economy grow, or be 'healthy', rather than there being any reason or ulterior driving motive, as there is no need for expanding production, as such, in the West. Even profit occurs 'elsewhere', as it is not reliant on real capital. In short, the economy no longer happens at the level of production. For Baudrillard, 1929 also sees the recognition of the productive nature of consumption (which in turn subsumes production), and the production of work as a function of this.

Industrial society manages scarcity, and the political aspect to this is democracy. Fundamental to democracy is the possibility of alternance. Baudrillard develops a leftist critique that so-called materialists would dispute: instead of asserting that whoever rules does it in favour of capital(ism), Baudrillard argues we cannot privilege the straightforwardly economic. Capitalism develops within a more general economy where the world is a product of representations, and its further 'material' developments also occur in 'thought'. Political alternance is part of a shift of the 'real' which also sees the development of the model of DNA and the genetic code, and also the binary code of information technology. Baudrillard writes of a general 'code', which replaces the quasi-Marxist term 'the system', as the code is what drives the system. This code is based on the code of DNA, which produces a range of forms – models – which could be almost infinitely varied, from a series of simple alternances. Baudrillard characterizes our culture as digitalized, and DNA as the crowning moment (*Symbolic Exchange*, p. 57; 89). Baudrillard's 'code', then, is all-pervasive yet indeterminate. Equally, all can be summoned up in/as the code, which operates via trial and error, question and response (p. 62; 96). If alternance is in the code, then there is no position of externality in 'radical' critique, to the extent that politically, the possibility of alternance between left and right demonstrates their interchangeability (*L'Échange symbolique*, p. 58).[3] There is no way out, no position that does not already carry its own assimilation or appropriation (in terms of mainstream political parties, we can see the adoption on what was the left of 'green' politics, on the right, the far-right ideas about control of immigration, or indeed left-wing ideas by right-wing parties and vice versa). Even with some form of symbolic exchange, there is no pure political action. Protests against globalization, which might seem close to what the 'early Baudrillard' saw as symbolic exchange, rely on the very phenomenon they are 'against', and in any case, are using tactics from another era. Furthermore, such protest belongs to simulation, as it shows the resurgence of a nostalgic take on anarchism, one that is superficial and mediated by right-wing libertarianism (it is, therefore, thoroughly appropriate to its time, and this is its limit).

The all-pervasiveness of the model/code pre-empts a resurgence of the real – for example, 'public opinion' replaces the opinions of people. Both 'public' and 'opinion' are simulation models, as is their pairing. We then see 'the impossibility of obtaining a *non-simulated* response to a *direct[ed]* question' (*Symbolic Exchange*, p. 67 trans. mod.; 103). This all-pervasiveness is not so new, but the result of the hollow triumph of the real, and simulated responses apply to the questionings of science (for example, the use of the particle accelerator to create the theorized particles which were 'present at the beginning', the invention of 'dark matter' because there isn't enough stuff in the universe): 'at the end of this process of reproducibility, the real is not only that which can be reproduced, but *that which is always already reproduced*: the hyperreal' (p. 73; 114).

The model/code is not one of exclusion (except with regard to symbolic exchange), but of incitement. So although the hyperreal is produced to a large extent in the media, it is *through*, not by the media, that we move to 'the end of the spectacle and the spectacular, towards the total, fusional, tactile and aesthesic (and no longer the aesthetic), environment' (p. 71; 111). This is like Artaud's vision of total theatre, writes Baudrillard, but instead of cruelty, we have stimulation in simulation. Although Baudrillard does not insist on this synaesthetic simulation (embracing all senses and annulling them as individual instances), it is an important gesture in dislocating the theory that would see the media as manipulation. This would be the case if a unilateral visual space of *reception* is maintained, that is that the media produce images, with the masses looking on as consumers. This hyperreal is the reproduction of the real from the model of the real, for example, the insistence on 'real-life programmes' on TV, fitness replacing health, sexuality, the 'voice of the people', 'natural' products and despairing authenticity: 'the real for its own sake, a fetishism of the lost object of representation, [but] the ecstasy of denegation and its own virtual extermination: the hyperreal' (p. 72; 112).

Reality is everywhere in the same way as the factory, prison or asylum, i.e. reality is produced in privileged sites of discourse (early versions of media), and spreads to define the entire system. A process of explosion turns in on itself: Baudrillard's figure of 'implosion'. This is the process whereby the code takes over from the oppositional logic of the order of production, from 'the distinction between cause and effect, between active and passive, between subject and object, between means and the end' (*Simulacra and Simulation*, p. 30 trans. mod.; 54). In the current situation:

> Nothing separates one pole from the other any more, the beginning from the end: there is just a kind of flattening out of one another, a fantastic telescoping, a collapse of the two traditional poles into each other: *implosion* – an absorption of the radiating mode of causality, of the differential mode of determination, with its positive and negative charge – an implosion of meaning. *That is where simulation begins.* (p. 31 trans. mod.; 55)

As opposed to certain commentators on the 'postmodern' (such as Lyotard and Jameson), who highlight theories of dispersal, Baudrillard envisages a collapse into *solidity*, density. Moreover, although the onset of simulation is difficult to place, this is due to there not being an original moment of transformation, as there is a succession of developments which make 'the change' quantitative as well as qualitative. Baudrillard's use of Borges's story of the imperial map, 'Of Exactitude in Science', is vital for showing us both where the real has gone, and that it does not entirely vanish in one fell swoop. Borges is relevant for simulation in general in that much of his writing takes place in situations which, unlike science fiction, do not assert or justify their otherness, but function as if they were true; there is no external reality to appeal to or fight against. Borges's stories are models that pre-empt the real. In fact, Borges's 'Of Exactitude in Science' can tell us more about simulation than Baudrillard makes it say.

In Borges's story, the narrator tells of an empire where extremely detailed maps are made, such that a map of a province is as large as a city. The cartographers are not content with the accuracy of these maps, and make one 'that was of the same Scale as the Empire and that coincided with it point for point' (*A Universal History of Infamy*, p. 131). Later inhabitants think this map excessive, and leave it to be destroyed by the weather. All that remains are fragments in the desert. It is not this map that stands for simulation, as the map is the attempt, at least, to represent the reality of the territory. For Baudrillard, in simulation, the priority is reversed, and it is the real whose fragments flap across the map. The map comes to stand for the model that tries to generate the real:

> It is the generation by models of a real without origin or reality: a hyperreal. The territory no longer precedes the map, nor does it survive it. As of now, it is the map that precedes the territory – *precession of simulacra* – that engenders the territory. (*Simulacra and Simulation*, p. 1 trans. mod.; 10)

Competing versions of reality and its representation are at issue in this encounter between Borges and Baudrillard. The latter has taken a superficial reading, in order to turn the story into an allegory of simulation (where it could be read as its opposite, due to the failure of the map), but he could equally have done more with it. Another reading could emphasize the futility of representation (with perhaps Baudrillard himself as one of those overseeing the destruction of the map), and then read Baudrillard's schema of simulacra into the progress of maps in the Empire of the story.[4] The Empire stands as a natural sign for the territory, implying identity with the latter by virtue of being an Empire, rather than a nation or State. The development of maps suggests the counterfeit

– the possibility of making a copy as good as the 'real' sign (the cartographers counterfeiting the development of the Empire itself by the Military, for example). The drive to total accuracy suggests that truth is possible, and can be *produced*. Finally, the map collapses when left to its own devices. In another reading, however, any map is already posing the problems of the 'era of production', where what is real can be faithfully represented. In this reading, the category of the map undermines any strict concordance between 'orders of simulacra' and historical shifts. I believe Baudrillard would only insist on such a link with regard to the onset of full simulation, which he takes to be the contemporary status of reality, and his use of Borges's story leads to the essential difference between representation and simulation, as the latter entirely subsumes the former.

Baudrillard recognizes that the story itself cannot function as a generator of simulation, and instead of making the story the map of his discourse (or vice versa), declares that it cannot function, as the 'sovereign difference' between map and reality has itself collapsed (ibid.). But perhaps 'Of Exactitude in Science' can better be enlisted to stand for the colonization of the real by the hyperreal, with the real outdoing itself, through the accuracy of representation. The map gradually spreads over the territory, and merges with it, and perhaps certain areas merge faster, the map catching hold more slowly elsewhere, where pockets of the real (or awareness of real/representation) persist.[5]

The persistence, or otherwise, of the real is a crucial element that has to be pieced together from Baudrillard's inferences and varied approaches to different simulacra. The loss of the gold standard is surely not sufficient to explain, or even describe the passage to hyperreality. Much of simulation, for Baudrillard, has come about due to the development of the mass media (following on from Benjamin's 'Work of Art in the Era of Mechanical Reproduction').[6] Essentially, for Baudrillard, our perception, and this time the world as such, are altered through technological advance that has allowed the media to become the map/territory. The media are like the code of DNA, the pre-emptive modelling of the real. That is not to say that they manipulate reality, as their operation precludes a space of manipulation ('there is no longer any medium in the literal sense' being Baudrillard's rewrite of McLuhan's 'the medium = the message', when now the medium has nothing to mediate). Kellner has a point when he writes of Baudrillard's 'media essentialism and technological determinism' (*Baudrillard*, p. 74) except for his insistence that Baudrillard fails to recognize the media's subordination to the 'forces of capital'. Some people, or institutions, do have more say than others in the direction of hyperreality, and seek to dominate the mediatized world. Such domination, though, does not preclude a change in the nature of the domination, such that control (with of course the realness of it) is itself threatened. At the same time, this control will appear even more real. Elsewhere, Baudrillard's text seems to allow Kellner's point, as his analysis replicates ideological critique: for instance, with regard to Watergate, the 'scandal' was not a scandal in the sense of being rare, puzzling or against the norm, but was something that served to legitimate the otherwise 'good' functioning of American democracy (*Simulacra and Simulation*, p. 15; 29). This applies equally to his analysis of the Vietnam War, where he argues that military victory over North Vietnam was not a priority as long as a 'stable government' could be formed, with which deals could be made, in preference to the incommensurability of the guerillas (p. 37; 63).

If Baudrillard is guilty of technological determinism, his excuse would no doubt be that it is specifically hyperreality that is technologically determined, that we have only now arrived at this, due largely to the propagation of the mass media. This (media) technology is what ensures the 'precession of simulacra', the precedence of simulation over all that already existed as real, and it is not technology as such that determines, but models, and part of this cannot be separated from advances in technology (the idea of the model being inextricably linked with production).[7] In other words, it is not only technology, but the alteration in perception that accompanies (*not* results from) it, that 'determines' our mode of perception. In particular, for Baudrillard, models come to dominate reality, rather than events in themselves. This parallels the processes of both mass production (especially with regard to media) and the coding of the real by science and the sign.

This precedence is in fact suggested by Baudrillard's version of the fate of history, including the future. The Vietnam War signals the beginning of the media's new role of being 'to maintain the illusion of an actuality' (p. 38; 65), a function which transforms into pre-emptive modelling of the war. This starts with Vietnam as it witnesses the combination of the newly all-pervasive media, along with the deviation of the traditional aim of war (i.e. to win). These combine in a hyperrealization of war, as the real is lost among images and strategic models. The two levels of simulation at work in the Vietnam War could be taken as inconsistency on the part of Baudrillard's theory, or alternatively (and I think, *despite* Baudrillard) as the fragments of the real that persist in the midst of simulation, as suggested in the following:

> moralists about war, champions of war's exalted values[8] should not be too upset: a war is no less terrible for being a mere simulacrum – the flesh suffers just the same, the dead and the veterans counting much the same (as dead and veterans in other wars). (pp. 37–8 trans. mod.; 64)

In other words, we can take it that even globalized hyperreality, which alters the status/actuality of war, does *not* prevent localized intrusions of reality. It is important to clarify that Baudrillard would not refer to 'American imperialism' bringing a reality to bear, for example, but that a violent real does subsist as a kind of fallout, as 'events continue at ground level . . . but subtly they no longer have any meaning' (p. 36; 62). As a result,

> one can completely miss the truth of a war: namely that it was finished well before reaching a conclusion, that there was an end to war at the heart of the war itself, and that perhaps it never even started. Many other events (the oil crisis, etc.) *never started*, never existed. (p. 38; 65)

This argumentation is used by Baudrillard in his analysis of the Gulf War in *The Gulf War*, and it is ignorance of Baudrillard's concept of a 'non-event' that led to the almost universal puzzled derision that greeted Baudrillard's contention that the Gulf War did not happen.[9]

In terms of history, the same process is at work, such that the future is consumed in advance ('The Year 2000 Will Not Happen'),[10] and the past is recycled as a 'hyperreal' or 'cool' past ('Holocaust', in *Simulacra and Simulation*, pp. 49–51; 77–80).

Baudrillard names this process 'deterrence', from nuclear deterrence. Nuclear deterrence takes the place of war – it is not destruction that 'paralyses' us, but deterrence, which is 'the neutral, implosive violence of metastable systems or systems in involution' (p. 32; 57). However, it does not seem to have stopped a continuous succession of wars around the 'un-deterred' world. Baudrillard argues that the whole planet gets brought into a 'hypermodel of security' (p. 33; 58). From this we can infer that wars fought by proxy between the US and the USSR occur as part of the maintenance of deterrence (although this returns us, against Baudrillard, to what seems to be an element of agency in the hyperreal). If we ask, then, what is the difference between real and hyperreal war, other than a systemic cynicism in the absence of motive, there seems to be little or no practical difference. However, even if war looks the same, an alteration in its status of reality has a huge bearing, as war becomes an *effect* of hyperreality, rather than an awkward stumbling point:

1. War can become a 'pure media event' – where all possibilities are exhausted in advance, both by 'official' and media strategists – one way in which the Gulf War did not happen, according to Baudrillard. In the case of that particular war, people did actually die, but this becomes irrelevant, as any reality of war is used up as a media event. The dead are no longer seen to matter.[11]

2. If we accept Baudrillard's problematization of causality, such that the purposes of (a) war become indeterminate, then a war without ends will not come to an end as a result of rational gains, and will instead take the course of pure violence as the sole model (e.g. aiming for the complete destruction of the enemy and/or their territory).

3. The hyperreal war may mean that a war *really* does not happen at all (pure deterrence), which, as with the Cold War, is actually perpetual war, even though it never has to break into real war. The existence of wars fought by proxy would take place, in this schema, in areas where the hyperreal is either not present, or that its status for *us*, within the blanket of deterrence, is hyperreal.

4. The two World Wars brought war to totality, and as with

prisons, the real or the sign, real war vanishes to become hyperreal – and the initiating point is the Holocaust as the removal of rational, real war.[12]

Baudrillard himself observes that 'the reality of simulation is unbearable' (p. 38; 66), confirming that hyperrealization of war in no way sanctions a view that 'it is only on TV' as TV and the real are merging. Against Baudrillard, I would argue that simulation is far from total, although it operates *as if* it were, and this is perhaps why the threat of 'real' war remains.

Baudrillard wrote this in the context of the Cold War (the above essay was first published in 1976), and although the global political situation is very different today, the argument remains at least as valid, as I aim to demonstrate in Chapter 4. Simulation gave shape to the Vietnam War, but the war also drove simulation on, such that it is not just our perceptions that are altering, but the structuring of perceptions is driving the real more completely than in any other era. One of the questions we might ask Baudrillard is whether simulation is total, and what seems specific to this era of simulacra is the globalization of a model of one unified world, linked or even made by communications. This completes the process initiated in 1929, with the collapse and then simulated survival of the previous capitalist system; continued with the spread of mass media, the impossibility of politics breaking out of 'the system' (or more accurately, awareness of this), and war as communications strategy.

Simulation, as theory and key problematic, never goes away in Baudrillard's work. It underpins all later work on the virtual, the event, the disappearance of reality, the various illusions about history. It does change slightly, however, with the addition of a fourth order of simulacra (after those of the counterfeit, of production and of simulation), and this is the fractal. Gane claims that this is a genuinely new stage (*In Radical Uncertainty*, pp. 22, 57–62), but other than Baudrillard's view on what might be new, nothing in what used to be called the real world seems to justify a newly hyperbolic epoch, so close on the heels of the last (which is still not complete). This is how Baudrillard outlines the term in 1990, which is to be the new fourth order:

Let me introduce a new particle into the microphysics of simulacra. For after the natural, commodity, and structural stages of value comes the fractal stage . . . At the fourth, the fractal (or viral, or radiant) stage of value, there is no point of reference at all, and value radiates in all directions, occupying all interstices, without reference to anything whatever. (*Transparency of Evil*, p. 5; 13)

In simulation, values exchanged among themselves, as if they were real, as if there were a reality, and this is what Baudrillard terms hyperreality. The new fractal dimension(s) is one where value becomes arbitrary: random and fixed at the same time. This means that all can become political, but not properly so, all can be sexual, but not fully, all can become economic or aesthetic. All of this occurs at the same time, and it becomes impossible to separate out previously discrete areas of human activity. TV is no longer content to 'show' reality, and thereby make the real more hyper-real, but now intervenes in events, puncturing the last illusion of a distinction between real and copy. The speed and level of technology mean that the world is one infinitely dispersed entity (or, more accurately, non-entity). This is what distinguishes even this phase from postmodernisms that emphasize the dispersal of old hierarchies and orders: what we have is properly fractal, and there is a whole that chaotically orders the dispersal. Individual ideas, ideologies, concepts, theories are also driven to endlessly reproduce, like viruses (*as* viruses), but with no ulterior purpose. There is, however, little textual presence of the fractal (i.e. Baudrillard does not seem to insist on it), and if it really has the status of a new order of simulacra (rather than being, as I would assert, a variant of the third),[13] then notions such as 'impossible exchange' do not fit a fractalized model of the world. The paradoxical duality of simulatedness against symbolic exchange never goes away (not without weakening the force of Baudrillard's newer theories anyway). That which appears on the 'outside', against simulation, but caught within its orbit, is the subject of the next chapter.

Notes

1. There is evidence that Baudrillard does intend this. The counterweight to a purely historical and one-dimensional 'progress' to simulation can be found in *Seduction*, where the Renaissance is not just part of the era of the counterfeit, but also of 'trompe-l'œil' – in some ways the model for the simulation we are currently supposed to inhabit (p. 86; 61). The text as a whole offers seduction as a form of mediation of simulation and symbolic exchange, but otherwise adds nothing to the 'theory of simulation' that I am taking as Baudrillard's main project.

2. Baudrillard reiterates that we have always had simulation in the essay 'Simulacra and Science Fiction' (*Simulacra and Simulation*, pp. 121–7; 177–86). The three orders of simulacra consist of 'natural simulacra'; then 'productive simulacra'; and finally, 'simulacra of simulation' (p. 121; 177).

3. This does not appear in the English translation.

4. The framing of the story mirrors the collapse of representation through fragmentation: it is an 'extract' from 'Travels of Praiseworthy Men (1658) by J.A. Suárez Miranda', and is as much a fragment of geography as the tatters of the Imperial map. Its status as an extract from a learned tome of the past also demonstrates the simulacritude of Borges's worlds, rather than their representationality.

5. Perhaps this has also 'really' happened, with the mapping of the entire world, and particularly with stylized, schematized, or 'functional' maps. Respectively: tourist, underground rail, and route maps.

6. Benjamin, 'The Work of Art in the Age of Mechanical Reproduction', in *Illuminations*, pp. 217–51. Benjamin argues that the era of mass mechanical reproduction changes the nature of works of art, which lose their 'aura' (authentic originality). The exemplary form of this is (the) film, which is exactly reproducible, and accessible to the masses. Although Benjamin took this development to signal a new site of cultural struggle, hints of Baudrillard's suspicion of 'reality everywhere' can (retrospectively) be seen: 'the adjustment of reality

to the masses and of the masses to reality is a process of unlimited scope' (p. 223). Benjamin took this to be the way in which the masses would know and then change reality, and Baudrillard not only attacks this spread of the real, but also characterizes the masses as a construct of implosion (*In the Shadow of the Silent Majorities*). Of at least equal importance for Baudrillard in this respect is the work of Marshall McLuhan. The term 'the medium is the message' (*Understanding Media*, p. 7) if nothing else, is a continual reference for Baudrillard's theory of simulation. McLuhan argues that the content is only another medium, such that the content of a film mediates writing, a story, characters, etc., all of which used to be dominant media in their own right (p. 18). Further illustration of the influence of McLuhan on Baudrillard can be seen in the following: 'After three thousand years of explosion, by means of fragmentary and mechanical technologies, the Western world is imploding' (p. 3). The site of this collapse shows the extent of its reach: 'The effects of technology do not occur at the level of opinions or concepts, but alter sense ratios or patterns of perception' (p. 18). Baudrillard has accepted much of what McLuhan claims, but the former's relation to Nietzsche and Bataille mediates this acceptance extensively.

7. It is not only technology that initiates simulation, and perhaps Baudrillard might argue that technology has no necessary bearing on simulation at all, if simulation is the question of the real/representation divide. Technology is the product of orders of simulacra, rather than vice versa.

8. For Baudrillard, this includes all those who attribute great importance to war one way or the other, and therefore includes those 'opposed' to war.

9. Norris, in particular, managed to fabricate a whole book based on a spectacular lack of reading, combined with wilful misreading on this point. See his *Uncritical Theory*. For a comprehensive critique of Norris's 'reading' of Baudrillard on the Gulf War, see William Merrin, 'Norris, Baudrillard and the Gulf War', *Economy and Society* 23 (4) (1994), pp. 433–58.

10. 'The Year 2000 Will Not Happen', in E.A. Grosz *et al.* (eds), *FuturFall: Excursions into Post-Modernity*, pp. 18–28. The original

title is 'L'an 2000 ne passera pas', and also appeared as 'The Year 2000 Has Already Taken Place' in Arthur and Marilouise Kroker (eds), *Body Invaders: Panic Sex in America*, pp. 35–44. 'Passer' could well suggest, as Baudrillard's text does, that it will not happen because it already has.

11. When Baudrillard first wrote the article 'La guerre du golfe n'aura pas lieu' ('The Gulf War will not take place'), Baudrillard seemed to *actually* think that there would be no war, although his many comments on war and simulation show that an event's not happening does not preclude all effects in the real world. This is why I have used 'pure' here. There is the further connotation that for the military, war can be conducted without scruple, with all the new techniques of projection, precision and threats of deployment. (See, for example, Clinton's threats of air strikes in Bosnia. When it came to it, the Bosnian Serbs did not acknowledge the precedence of simulation, and challenged the US to 'get real', a challenge it refused.) This perception is an integral part of the precession of simulacra (which Baudrillard himself was taken in by), and the consequence is that when war does happen, the models are believed (such as 'surgical strikes' and 'smart bombs' successfully wiping out enemy targets with the minimum of force), and control the functioning of the war at all levels of 'reality'.

12. The mass murder was itself conducted with stark rationality, for the most part. The horror of the Holocaust in theoretical terms is that it is somewhere around the limit of the rational – did it occur because of or despite rationality? Genocide in Cambodia or Rwanda, for example, will never stimulate the same reaction, partly because of the belief in rationality as fundamentally good, and that if genocide happens outside of the padded cell of Reason, it is because 'they' have not progressed, but we have.

13. Rex Butler goes further, and writes that the fractal order 'is in fact no different from the third' (*Jean Baudrillard: The Defence of the Real*, p. 46).

Chapter 3

Other than Simulation

If earlier orders of simulacra require an exclusion of symbolic exchange, and have otherness, death and the outside as threat, then simulation as *the* all-inclusive system must also be threatened by the possibility of its own limit. At a certain point (in the midst of *Simulacra and Simulation*, perhaps), the real ceases to be an issue in Baudrillard's text (and so does simulation). This move instigates the shift away from the explicit use of symbolic exchange as a term, but the problem of the relation between symbolic exchange and simulation remains unresolved for Baudrillard. The texts following those that theorize simulation seem to reside in this problematic space. On the one hand, we see this transfer or slide into simulation being accounted for, and on the other, simply ignored, as the problematic no longer applies when simulation is in place.

Seduction comes to replace symbolic exchange, occupying the same position *across* simulation (i.e. it is not simply other to it), but unlike symbolic exchange, it is not a rupture of the real, but a sliding threat that is also *in* simulation. This is due to seduction working not against simulation, but as the inspiration for the installation of simulacra of all types, as these are the response to the 'mystery' of appearances. Symbolic exchange is superseded, and seduction is now the *différantial* movement that establishes the 'true' (this is not a historical, but a theoretical succession within Baudrillard). Seduction is the term that allows Baudrillard to account for the world of appearances, and its fascination for us. The various stages of simulation use appearance, but try to master and limit it, making what we see more real all the time, and when that is all you see, you have hyperreality, not a genuine reality.

Although seduction seems a different principle altogether, in the overall economy of Baudrillard's thought, seduction is the pursuit of symbolic exchange by other means. Seduction is, in turn, one of a series of terms that will haunt the system of simulation: 'On the one hand: political economy, production, the code, the system, simulation. On the other hand: potlatch, expenditure, sacrifice, death, the feminine, seduction, and in the end, the fatal' (*Ecstasy*, p. 79; 69). In the 1990s and early 2000s, we will also see the return of the threat of symbolic exchange in the form of 'Evil', and also in the form of 'impossible exchange'. Seduction itself re-occurs, recast in 'illusion'. As well as seduction, which marks the move from even a suggestion of a place beyond simulation, this chapter will address the following terms: symbolic violence, the fatal, evil, illusion (including the notion of the perfect crime) and impossible exchange. On the one hand, as I am claiming here, these terms are variants of the same thing, but, on the other, they mark a progression away from agency, and towards the unpredictable, the accidental, the violent, the catastrophic, as the only things between us and total hyperreality.

Seduction

For Baudrillard, seduction stands for play, the play of appearances which has always prevented the existence of a transparent reality, which would be free from the traps of illusion, while *allowing* simulation of truth to operate. Its operation is curtailed in the 'obscenity' of simulation, where the excess of reality (hyperreality) pre-empts the reversibility of seduction, while seeming to offer it. TV, for example, offers so many choices, we can only accept its invitation to play. This 'is a source of fascination. But one can no longer speak of a sphere of enchantment or seduction; instead an era of fascination is beginning' (*Seduction*, p. 158; 216). Seduction implies sexuality, but eroticism and play have given way to visibility and omnipresence, everything is now sexualized, 'register[ing] an explicit demand for seduction, but a soft seduction, whose weakened condition has become synonymous with so much else in this society – the ambience, the manipulation, the persuasion, the gratification, the strategies of desire' (p. 178; 243). It is precisely in this era of 'seduction's simulation' (p. 178; 244) that seduction shows itself as other than simulation.

Seduction seems to offer Baudrillard a better version of symbolic exchange, as it is in 'the order . . . of artifice' (*Seduction*, p. 2; 10), and is free of a claim to primordial truth, while offering an account of an earlier simulacrum, or pre-simulacrum perhaps, with dissimulation preceding simulation. This is the first time he suggests the possibility of there being something other than simulacra which always seek positivity, that is, seek to become systems of truth. Now we have the possibility of the 'more false than false' (pp. 60, 94; 86, 130). Previously, his theories have concentrated on the production/appearance of the real, truth, or fixed values, all of which seemed beyond appeal. Seduction is specifically opposed to production, and the two are set up as Manichean world processes, such that '*seduction* is that which is everywhere and always opposed to *production*' (*Forget Foucault*, p. 21; 27). This is not a standard binary opposition, as it is production only that insists on such: 'seduction is not that which is *opposed to* production. It is that which *seduces* production – just as absence is not that which is opposed to presence' (*Ecstasy*, p. 58; 52). Nonetheless, there is an appearance of opposition, and the sense of a world outside production (where production is of truth, reality and is a unilateral, irreversible process). Echoing both his own *Mirror* and Foucault's *History of Sexuality*, Baudrillard discusses the production of sexual subjects, as this production is central to modern society, and to attempts to change the controls imposed in that world. However, seduction is a concept that troubles the centrality of sexuality as truth, in order to get at truth itself, and valorize open-ended processes and appearances. Seduction is an 'ironic, alternative form, one that breaks the referentiality of sex and provides a space, not of desire, but of play and defiance' (*Seduction*, p. 21; 38).

There is a shift to the fundamental untruth of the universe, world or reality. Any sense of reality we have, or any challenges to this come from the perpetual struggle between forms of seduction and forms of production. That this is an ontological argument, and not simply one about how we know or represent the world, is both its strength and weakness. It clarifies Baudrillard's 'grounding' (i.e. the world, reality, symbolic exchange, even, do not have one), but, in so doing, presents what seems to be an ahistorical model.[1] Overall, the model of simulation does not require seduction formulated in this way, as simulation was already an ambiguous ontological model, not just one about the history of representation. In it, reality is a result of 'representations', and nothing else. The theory of seduction, in proposing a mischievous version of appearances suggests that there is a real world to be fought over and defined, even if we never know the world itself (as in the following statement: 'seduction as a mastering of the reign of appearances opposes power as a mastery of the universe of meaning' (*Ecstasy*, p. 62; 55)).

Seduction comes to occupy a highly privileged position as a near-universal term, original rather than originary, due to the removal of a sense of a (retrospective) breach suggested in symbolic exchange: 'seduction is inescapable' (*Seduction*, p. 42; 65); 'everything is seduction and nothing but seduction' (p. 83; 115); 'seduction is destiny' (p. 180; 247). As a principle, seduction is diffuse, opaque, deadly and playful, so it is not simply a question of seduction being the final truth, although there are hints of this. The second of the three quotations above is a rewriting of the last line of Nietzsche's *The Will to Power*, proclaiming the nothingness of the world, as all that there is 'will to power' (§1067). In the context of symbolic exchange and its termination in simulation, the problem that arises with the use of seduction is that Baudrillard can now close off the possibility of the ambiguous, death, or the *défi* (challenge) as being the possibility of an opening to an (unattainable) outside. *Le défi* does provide a ground for resistance, but seems both too blatant (it is always 'against') and too limited. In a way similar to his replication of the exclusion of death that he seeks to criticize (making it the excluded other) when he writes on Bataille's general economy, Baudrillard now repeats the 'strategy of the real' with his pairing of simulation and seduction, i.e. all will be realized, and there will be no outside, because for all the play and challenge offered by seduction, any success is mitigated by remaining in the realm of appearances. Baudrillard criticizes simulation for removing play, challenge, and so on, only to remove it himself in installing seduction as a total, *constant* and *contained* Other.

The Other I have not yet mentioned that is central to the theory of seduction, is Woman and/or the feminine. Seduction is Baudrillard's take on sexuality (alongside the numerous dismissals of psychoanalytic fetishization of same) as well as being a theory of appearances. It can be taken as being very conservative, or as matching certain of the theories (and the style) of Irigaray, or later writers such as Judith Butler. It really comes down to whether you want to criticize or, as Victoria Grace does, in *Baudrillard's Challenge*, use the theory.

Baudrillard argues that sexual liberation of women is the wrong avenue for women to go down, as it is the end of any vestiges of sexuality, or indeed the feminine, and brings all together into a knowable, productive system (*Seduction*, p. 5; 15). One example of what was relatively new in the late 1970s and went on to become more widespread in the 1980s, is the scientization of sex itself, along with the insistence on an individual's right to an orgasm (p. 17; 32). In short, Baudrillard maintains that feminist or quasi-feminist arguments for a greater awareness and enhancement of women's sexual experience are part of a process of limiting women, who had previously existed in the realm of seduction, and not production (p. 8; 19). The feminine is about appearance, and it disrupts the masculine/feminine polarity (which is a masculine construct) (p. 12; 25). The masculine is the world of truth, reality and results (orgasm). The feminine is that which escapes, remains unknown.[2] It is a 'duel and agonistic relation' (p. 105; 145), and is in both the seducing and the being seduced (p. 81; 112). Much of this could come from what would be dubbed 'écriture féminine', and we should be wary of reading Baudrillard any differently because of his biology. The argument could be made that his take on sexuality is as problematic or as successful as Irigaray's (early) work, and that it largely valorizes 'the feminine'.

However, there are moments when we have to question Baudrillard's position on women. As well as casually made statements about women inventing seduction techniques for men (p. 86; 118), women being nearer to seduction as men have access to depth (p. 68; 97), and women being about appearance, we have the problematic notion of valorizing woman as object. Baudrillard offers a very clear critique of pornography, arguing that it is synonymous with simulation, where all must be made visible (see pp. 25–31;

43–51). Seduction plays with appearances, though, and women (as avatars of 'Woman') take their revenge in exaggerating their position as sex objects. For Baudrillard, the status of object is the radical one (p. 92; 126), and, in fact, it is the object that has become feminine more than the feminine an object (p. 27; 45). Feminism, of course, would not agree, arguing that real women suffer as a result of this objectification. But just as with his arguments about simulated war not being any less dangerous for being less real, the 'reality' of the situation is not what's at stake here. There has been a rise in the commercial and/or visual sexualization of women, and many (outside the world of academic discourse) claim that this time, in certain areas of the West, at least, it is as voluntarily selected as the wearing of 'revealing' clothing in the 'real world'. Very powerful women performers choose to take their sexualization and throw it back doubled (such as Missy Elliott). Are contemporary women closer to thinking like Baudrillard than to feminism? Alternatively, have they bought into a double simulation of: (1) feminism as freedom; (2) sexuality as freedom?

Coming slightly closer to a feminist take, Baudrillard offers hysteria and anorexia as ultimate examples of seduction (p. 121; 167). They offer themselves (or 'present') as symptoms, only to lure the psychoanalyst into believing there is meaningful depth, rather than the 'superficial abyss' (p. 54; 79) of seduction. Psychoanalysis in fact does create a meaning, and compounds its initial mistake in dragging the seducing hysteric into the realm of production (a further inevitable mistake is to read seduction here in its limited form and imagine that the 'symptom-producer' is trying to appeal to the analyst or to anyone else).[3] Pro-anas (pro-anorexics), for example, would concur that their appearance is not about the fantasies of psychoanalysis. Baudrillard, however, might not see their stance as an endorsement, as it could be seen as very literal-minded, and an attempt to valorize what was before (valorization) a radical non-position.

The theory of seduction veers between a 'French feminist' position and a highly conservative, dated view of women. It also tends towards being a critique of sexuality (at all levels) as it actualizes and diminishes seduction. The challenge of seduction is a challenge to the real to oppose it, to try to incorporate it. Any particular seduction might succumb, but the principle of a radical, unprincipled, seductive resistance, or revolt, remains. Baudrillard even offers a suggestion that is very close to the body art of the 1980s, which persists today in a state of technological excitation about bodily modifications, virtual bodies, the 'posthuman' wherein we can actualize our disappearance. He writes that disguise and dissimulation are the way to counter simulation. Instead of hiding from computerized surveillance, for example, you could opt for puzzling the 'system': 'seduction as an invention of stratagems, of the body, as a disguise for survival, as an infinite dispersion of lures, as an art of disappearance and absence, as a dissuasion which is stronger yet than that of the system' (*Ecstasy*, p. 75; 65–6).

Symbolic violence

This term differs from seduction and from the others that come later insofar as it is the principle that links the various phenomena that might elude simulation. It is also ambiguous, operating equally to stamp out non-simulated forms, which is in fact how we first encounter the idea in Baudrillard. It also signals the loss of agency that resistance can have: symbolic violence is submitted to rather than controlled (as we will see in Baudrillard's analysis of 9/11). Symbolic violence is initially the destruction of an idealized symbolic exchange. The (rational, capitalist) system 'lives on symbolic violence' (*Symbolic Exchange*, p. 36; 62), and this is more than the system being based on a founding violence, since this is a base which must persist for it to be seen as the original base. Symbolic violence is, at the same time, seen to have occurred within symbolic exchange. There is, then, a sense of this violence surrounding the question of origins, which makes symbolic violence reversible, a sort of hinge:

> symbolic violence is deduced from a logic of the symbolic (which has nothing to do with the sign or with energy): reversal, the incessant reversibility of the counter-gift and conversely, the seizing of power by the unilateral exercise of the gift. (p. 36; 63)

The 'system' (our culture, especially in capitalism) institutes the gift, giving it an independence it does not possess in 'primitive' society, bringing a fixity of hierarchy, accumulation, the social, exclusion of death – all those things that exist in the annulling of (their) reversibility (ibid.). In other words, our culture has sought to remove the aspects of challenge, counter-gift, reciprocity and so on, in favour of a unilateral, and therefore violent, gift, of work (primarily). The ultimate success of capitalism is in making its 'enemy', the proletariat and its later avatars, ask for or even demand work. The relations that constitute capitalism (broadly speaking) specifically prevent the re-emergence of a general, irruptive, sacrificial economy. At the same time, this annulled factor comes to permeate the unilateral (the irreversible), and as with death, symbolic violence remains constant both internally, and as fear of the excluded. This double nature of symbolic violence, along with the persistence of the *défi*, is set out by Baudrillard in the following passage:

> There must no longer be this direct possibility of symbolic confrontation taking place. All must be negotiated. And this is the source of our profound boredom. This is why taking hostages and other similar acts rekindle some fascination: they are at once an exorbitant mirror for the system of its own repressive violence, and the model of a symbolic violence which is always forbidden it, the only violence it cannot exert: that of its own death. (p. 38 trans. mod.; 65–6)

We are left with an omni-absent term (symbolic exchange) bringing the absence of absence (orders of simulacra, especially the third order, that of simulation) in the form of realnesses (varying according to the orders of simulacra), in other words, what Derrida identifies as the inevitable play of absence and presence that establishes and undermines the apparent solidity of the 'proper' (*propre*), this being identity in the shape of the self, the same or the truth.

Baudrillard talks of May 1968 as symbolic violence (*Simulacra and Simulation*, p. 151; 217), as something which sets the reversibility of power, or knowledge in play, as a reversal of the violence that installs the unilaterality of power at both cultural and theoretical levels. Symbolic violence is the site of the switch from Void to Value, and vice versa. This making of a limit (always seen in hindsight) will remain the closure of the possible from the Impossible, and as this limit will persist as limit, even if its form changes, symbolic violence can also stand for the re-opening of (making of) the limit.

The consideration of the double nature of symbolic violence returns briefly in *Forget Foucault*, even if the principal point of interest – the reversibility of power that Baudrillard argues Foucault has forgotten – is a replaying of the formulation of symbolic violence, itself intimately linked to seduction, 'a circular and reversible process of challenge, one-upmanship and death' (p. 48; 65). A system founded by symbolic violence is a system *of* symbolic violence. At the political level, this could perhaps be illustrated by the French Revolution (among others). The Revolution forcibly demarcates what is to be allowed from what is not, and signals the values (Reason, Democracy, Equality) that are appropriate, however, in the shape of the Terror, the Revolution is also paradigmatic of the crossing of the boundaries between Reason and its other, and is a condensation of what is a constant, reversible process.[4] Symbolic violence is mentioned as that which surrounds, initiates and threatens all other forms of violence or unilaterality (anything that insists on its own uniqueness as truth or reality). It is also important to note that rather than this violence ending with the onset of simulation, it is in some ways exposed (even if only as impossibility) to its own danger of reversal and by its precarious victory:

> we need precisely to grasp the radical lack of definition in the notion of the political, its lack of existence, its simulation, and what, from that point on, sends the mirror of the void back to power. Symbolic violence is more powerful than any political violence. (*Forget Foucault*, pp. 57–8 trans. mod.; 79)[5]

All that is outside simulation, even if only partially so, is driven by symbolic violence, having been outlawed as symbolically 'bad', and also with a process of symbolic violence, as outlined here, that consists of reversibility.

The fatal

Reversibility continues in the form of the Object. This has come a long way from being something essentially there to be categorized

for Baudrillard (see *Ecstasy*, pp. 77–95; 67–82). Now it is the location of 'the fatal', and represents *in itself*, immanently, a challenge
to subjects, the world of subjects and the drive to bring all into
reality. The Object is reversible, it has a 'fatal reversibility', writes
Baudrillard (*Fatal Strategies*, p. 72; 80). Exactly how an object is
reversible is never stated, which indicates we have to take the Object
as something other than objects, initially, at least. The object world
is habitually seen as that which is present to subjects. Science (and
the secular world) exists to know the object, the thing that exists
(comes to exist) for it. This object can also be in human form (as in
Foucault's *Discipline and Punish*), or it can be the masses, and/or the
form of humanity created by surveys, focus groups, market
research, charts, fashion. But, asks Baudrillard, what if the object
refused to continue being the passive recipient of knowledge's gaze?
What if the object is not subordinate, but able to drive an unfath-
omable dialectic, which constantly eludes the subject/science/sim-
ulation? Even in pure science, matter resists the closer it is observed
(*Fatal Strategies*, p. 84; 92). Partly what he has in mind is quantum
mechanics, and phenomena such as the endless breakdown of
matter into smaller and smaller constituent parts, but also the game
played by the object: science cannot just observe what is truly there,
because nothing is truly there. Science endlessly creates particles,
for example, in order to find them (literally, if we think of particle
accelerators such as CERN). If we look at astrophysics or cosmology, we see an endless array of ramshackle solutions as to the beginning, end, size, direction, momentum of the universe. Sokal and
Bricmont, in their rant against contemporary theory (*Intellectual
Impostures*), seem unaware of cosmology's twists and turns, and
attack Baudrillard for specious use of scientific terms such as black
holes or hyperspace, but we can take numerous examples (such as
those) to illustrate that astrophysics is an operational simulation.
    One phenomenon which I think encapsulates Baudrillard's line
of attack here is dark matter. Quite simply, apparently, the universe
is not massive enough: there is not enough stuff. One ingenious solution to this is the theory of dark matter, which we cannot perceive,
but is everywhere. Once invented, the gravitational pull of dark
matter could be observed. Maybe it does exist, but to believe we have
advanced in terms of knowing what is true is our (the contemporary

West's) driving myth. The only advance we have actually experienced is in the shape of the belief that our assessments of the world are ever more accurate. The world, though, offers itself ironically, or even humorously. Even DNA plays a game with us: it involves colossal time and research, and is still short of answers which might be usable or 'relevant'. Even then, there might be other things which pre-empt DNA as 'the secret of life'. Or, it may be that DNA itself is needlessly complicated, always opening more mysteries. *It* provides the resistance, in any case.

At a more everyday level, the object – in the form of the masses, the surveyed, the monitored – resists in several ways. We can of course lie to surveys, a phenomenon on the increase in recent years (one example being the British general election of 1992), and if this occurs in opinion polls, we can not only influence the outcome, we can make it irrelevant, or shift the purpose of the actual vote (as in the French elections of 2002, where the presidential election came to be about 'defending the republic' against the fascism of the Front National, and the ensuing general elections about giving that 'mission' a majority). But there are more passive ways to 'resist', and this is what Baudrillard has in mind by 'fatal strategy'. A recurring theme in *Simulacra and Simulation*, *In the Shadow* and *Fatal Strategies* is the manner in which the masses' passivity wrecks polls. The masses become inert, fully receptive and unwilling to choose – this is their revenge on the system that created them (masses here does not imply a class, but an object that is first subordinate to surveys, etc., but then begins a process of reversibility). They then follow instructions, and overload the system, for example, if exhorted to buy certain products at Christmas, or concert tickets as quickly as possible. Baudrillard's best example concerns the tedium of holidays. We should not be puzzled that everyone goes to the same place, or does pretty much the same as if at home, as this is 'surbanalité', the more banal than the banal (*Fatal Strategies*, pp. 184–5; 204–5). The masses also love the spectacle, rather than being oppressed or alienated by it (ibid.). Those who hope to leave commercialization behind are so alienated they think an authentic world exists that would be better than the spectacle (which has lost its autonomous existence).

A major source of spectacle is the accident, whether a car crash or a disaster somewhere not too close, but brought near by the media. Intellectuals console themselves with the spectacle of those enjoying the spectacle. But the accident is a phenomenon in its own right, and brings us to the 'fatal' itself. When events occur, we have two possible, habitual responses: either it is a result of chance, or we can clearly see a rational progression to the event. Both of these absolve us of responsibility or involvement, in valorizing an objective, neutral world. But, writes Baudrillard, there is no such thing as chance (*Fatal Strategies*, pp. 150–1; 167–8). Chance is an invention of a secularizing world, and is more about probabilities; it concerns calculations of likeliness, rather than any true random-ness.[6] Having said that, we still hope (or fear) a world where these probabilities do not apply, albeit momentarily (p. 153; 171). This is fate or destiny (*le destin*). If, for example, we are playing the lottery, we do not really want the odds of millions to 1 to actually apply. Instead we seek a sequence of mysterious yet inevitable events that lead to the moment where the one person is you. This is the differ-ence between true 'chance', which is fate, and the spurious chance of probabilities: fate happens to you, rather than just happening (pp. 159–60; 178). So, similarly, we hope lightning does not hit us, or a large meteor strike the earth. We do not want to live in a world dominated by fate. It is this inevitability of fate that interests Baudrillard: we can no longer be agents in the face of it: the chain of events will have come to be unavoidable, rather than always having been predictable. The ultimate figure of this is 'the cata-strophe' (which later texts refer to as 'the event'). This is not an accidental occurrence, but the product of a chain of events both necessary and irreducible to statistics, and this is the greatest chal-lenge 'the Object' offers us (pp. 155–6; 173–4).

We are not to do anything to resist this challenge, and quies-cence, in its turn, changes nothing. We can adopt strategies which resonate with the fatalness of the world, which other societies and other periods of history have done, in the form of ritual, as ritual offers a sort of counter-challenge (as in the counter-gift of sacrific-ing to the Sun). It removes agency, substituting rules for Law, and re-enacts a symbolic violence: 'ceremonial violence appears not as transgression, but as an exacerbation of the rule, where the whole world is suspended in the interruption of the game' (p. 169; 188).

Unlike the real, which is known, or to be known, rules, ritual and ceremony are immanent (p. 170; 189). The symbolic violence is reversible in the straightforward sense (changing direction), as well as being that which initiates or closes off reversibility itself (which is the 'possibility' of the seemingly impossible non-existence of a system that considers itself all-encompassing). Nothing is controlled in this summoning of symbolic violence, as the fatal is not even accepted. It is, merely.

Evil

In *Symbolic Exchange*, Baudrillard wrote about the exclusion of death, which finally becomes total in simulation (as it is hidden away, denied, or, alternatively, mediatized). He extends this, notably in *The Transparency of Evil*, to the attempt to deny any existence to evil. He argues that simulated society only knows Good, and as a result we are overprotected. Our exclusion of Evil, though, leads to its virulent return (*Transparency*, p. 65; 72). It is our positivity, our insistence on health and life as ultimate 'goods' that will bring our downfall. This positivity can be seen in the form of illnesses, where, as a result of antibiotics, we have 'superbacteria' (hyperbacteria?), and, most specifically, AIDS. When we talk of resistance to a simulated or virtual world, the resistance is coming from outside our control. But at another level, our politics have become about the management of 'good' phenomena, where 'rights' are paramount. This is something Baudrillard is scathing about: 'if a right must be demanded, it means that the battle is already lost' (p. 87; 94). We end up asking for things that are either so minimal as to be irrelevant (the right to 'be myself'), or actually a trick (the right to work). But fundamentally, the right-demander has misjudged where or how they actually are. In contemporary (postmodern – he uses the word here) society,

> The individual is a self-referential and self-operating unit. Under such circumstances, the human-rights system becomes totally inadequate and illusory: the flexible, mobile individual of variable geometric form is no longer a subject with rights but has become, rather, a tactician and promoter of his own existence whose point of reference is not

some agency of law but merely the efficiency of his own functioning or performance. (p. 87; 94)

This is a viral subject, constituted in networks, and largely without any control of his or her own activity. This is Deleuze and Guattari without the utopianism. The viral, or the fractal, is everywhere. Although Baudrillard argues that the problem with the simulated world is its insistence on unilateral Good, this good is not really something good (p. 6; 14), as we are in a banal version of Nietzsche's 'beyond Good and Evil' (p. 70; 77), where the two permeate each other. In fact, our attempts to stamp out all that threatens are what bring the 'transparency of Evil'. The transparency here is to do with appearing everywhere, rather than being visible as Evil. This type of transparency is brought on by the other, relentlessly positive form: all organizations insist on 'transparency', which of course has created extra levels of control and a re-establishment of a Foucauldian world that would otherwise have disappeared (see *Illusion*, p. 82; 120). We are also interested in openness in all ways (there can never be any resistance to this term) as closed is bad.

There is a great emphasis placed on valuing difference, but Baudrillard sees difference as a con, arguing that 'difference is what destroys otherness' (*Transparency*, p. 127; 131). It is not only a patronizing conceit, it is actually oppression by other means: 'for "we respect the fact that you are different" read: "you people who are underdeveloped would do well to hang on to this distinction because it is all you have left"' (p. 132; 137).[7] The insistence of a right to difference encapsulates two simple impositions (rights, 'difference'). In fact, what we end up with is a sort of conceptual globalization, one where *indifference* is the product (*Illusion*, p. 108; 151–2).

The net result of this is that the system is not ready for attack, as it cannot understand someone not being 'for' Good. But there are all kinds of resistances, some at the level of actual viruses, medical or electronic. Some occur at the level of political violence, and notably take the form of terrorism (discussed in Chapter 4), but there is also 'the catastrophe', which echoes the notion of 'the fatal', as it is the moment any presumed agency breaks down, returning to the object world (in this sense a natural disaster and a terrorist act are more or less the same thing). Our belief, in the form of ecological awareness, or better still 'concern', that nature is good is only a belief. Nature is malevolent, arbitrary (*Illusion*, p. 81; 119), and as 'object' has perhaps begun playing tricks on science, leading us to believe we are mastering nature in a way unheard of since the Garden of Eden (where the mastery was itself, at best, illusory).

Evil is a principle that is produced within all these realms, and as a principle it is unconnected to Good, emerging instead as a form of Bataille's 'accursed share'. Western society has continued to repel the idea that something must be sacrificed, that the principle of waste and destruction be acknowledged, but 'anything that purges the accursed share in itself signs its own death warrant' (*Transparency*, p. 106; 111). Historically, 'the energy of the accursed share, and its violence, are expressions of the Principle of Evil' (ibid.), but, as noted above, we live in a society that seeks to annul this energy. We are in the absence of the accursed share (but this absence was already a vital part of Bataille's theory). Evil is the filling up of the system by what it rejects, this time more dangerously than before. So is that to be encouraged, should we be more evil? I do not think that is the way Baudrillard sees Evil working – Evil is precisely the failure of rational control and action. It is a reversible phenomenon, permeating 'Good transparency' without interacting with it (p. 139; 144). Evil occurs as anomaly, catastrophe, symbolic violence, even as seduction, but it is no longer anything we can have anything to do with: evilness is radically other, not because it is always someone else we judge to be evil, but because it is outside all assimilation:

> The principle of Evil is not a moral principle but rather a principle of instability and vertigo, a principle of complexity and foreignness, a principle of seduction, a principle of incompatibility, antagonism and irreducibility. It is not a death principle – far from it. It is a vital principle of disjunction. (p. 107; 112)

Illusion

Simulation cannot be fought by recourse by truth; instead, it has to be exceeded. This could take the form of hypersimulation, or, with less reliance on agency,[8] illusion. In *The Perfect Crime*, Baudrillard outlines a very Nietzschean scheme of the history of illusion (echoing, not for the first time, *The Twilight of the Idols* and *The Will to Power*). All we have is illusion, there is nothing beyond that: 'there is no will. There is no real. There isn't something. There is nothing. Or, in other words, the perpetual illusion of an ungraspable object and the subject who believes he grasps it' (*The Perfect Crime*, p. 14; 31). This applies from the beginning, an unfindable origin, just like the Big Bang (and just as mythical) (p. 2; 14), and this is exacerbated through the course of Western history, only to find itself undone in the era of high technology and the insistence on the real that comes with it (p. 64; 95 and *passim*). But, without illusion there is nothing, and nothing is where we are headed.

The 'perfect crime' is the 'murder' of the 'vital illusion' of the world (p. i; 10): it is a crime because it is a destruction, and it is perfect because it has always already occurred, has no motives, no possible suspects and almost nothing by way of clues (p. ii; 11).[9] At the same time, though, this moment of the 'perfect crime' is when illusion comes to be. While this thought is much more philosophically argued than usual, it is also more obscure than usual. At the back of this idea is first of all the notion that there is no real reality. For the moment, let's just say 'nothing is real' (this idea itself, according to Baudrillard is also an illusion/myth). Human existence arrives with illusion, with the sense that death matters, that we think, act logically, have a memory, or whatever original myth you prefer. The illusion is not false, but necessary. It is necessary because the real world, in its non-existence, would be unbearable (p. 7; 20–1), but more importantly, there is no decision to be made: illusion has happened (or not) already, it is necessary because it has been. So we can move on from the simple nihilist position of 'nothing is real' because for Baudrillard, illusion *is*. This does not mean it is true – rather, everything is not true – and without this, nothing. But that nothing has no meaning: the moment humans exist and recognize nothingness, it too is illusion. If you remove humans, there still would not be any truth or reality.

From the basic 'illusion of the world', we move on to build others: deities, forces of nature, moral systems. Once in a society based on progress, linear time and endpoints, these illusions cause the progressive decline of illusion itself: science brings the real, and annuls illusion (even if it ironically perpetuates it by continually opening up areas yet to be real, known, controllable (p. 74; 109)). Baudrillard suggests that because illusion is all there is (or might be – you can't tell with illusion), then what we have is not a battle between real and illusion, but one between two types of illusion:

> [the vital illusion is] the illusion of appearances, of the forms of becoming, of the veil, and indeed all the veils which, happily, protect us from the objective illusion, the illusion of truth, from the transparent relation of the world to an objective truth, from the transparent relation of man to his own truth. This is the illusion of meaning, secreted by man when he takes himself to be the subject of history and the world. To which we can only oppose the *illusion of the world itself.* (*Illusion*, p. 94; 135)

One type, or mode, is the better one, the one that knows it is illusion. The other – making everything appear, making everything transparent – will remove all possibility for manoeuvre. All utopias, dreams and new ideas will disappear, but also so will things taken to be fundamental, such as death or the body (p. 95; 136). Without illusion, nothing changes, and the static real wins. This situation is specific to this era – one of complete transparency and visibility, one where speech is monitored, movements increasingly subject to surveillance, and your identity is not constructed by yourself or even anyone else's ideological system, but through your digital presence in the 'world'.

The early twenty-first century sees us stumbling slowly into a virtual world. The virtual aspires to be the real, completes the perfect crime, perfectly, while representing us taking possession of the crime (*The Perfect Crime*, pp. 109–10; 155–6). The virtual is occurring in all our attempts to replicate, and not just in the possible virtual IT environments, so this includes cloning, for example. With cloning, the illusion (the mythical, undoubted actuality) of immortality gives way to a real version, now (*Illusion*, p. 90; 131). But this is not genuine immortality, even if it might be real. This is a simulation, and a further illustration that simulation, in Baudrillard's world never equates with falsity.

Baudrillard suggests, occasionally, that we can do something about this: the artist is able to re-iterate, always for the first time, the perfect crime (*The Perfect Crime*, p. 1; 13); we can try to go along with the 'world illusion' rather than insist on reality (which feeds simulation) (*Illusion*, p. 94; 135). Overall, though, and more logically consistently, he argues that illusion is 'objective' (*The Perfect Crime*, p. 54; 80), that it has nothing to do with a choice, a use, a strategy. Strategy, and the capacity for strategy, have been taken back by the world. Theory has to realize this and not believe it can have a critical position, but offer illusions, seductions, paradoxes, even what might seem evil.

Impossible exchange

In recent works, we see a mutation of the 'perfect crime', in the form of the idea of 'impossible exchange'. Like the perfect crime, it has constantly underpinned 'reality' (i.e. what we have taken, in different ways, through history, to be reality), and is being exacerbated in recent times, in simulation. Impossible exchange is a more dynamic concept than the perfect crime; it is dualistic, threatening and possibly beneficial, real and not real. It is both the culminating point of the (simulated) real and of radical illusion. Impossible exchange is a radical situation brought about by simulation, and then seen to have always been there. With the drive to transparency, the world becomes real, and once it is fully real, there is nothing outside, nothing to exchange against (*Impossible Exchange*, p. 3; 11). What this means is that there is no more referential world, not even the simulation of a referential world. Nor is there any way of judging the truth of appearances. Values now have to exchange with 'Nothing' (*le Rien*); in other words, an endless, pointless relation. This applies to phenomena such as 'the economy', which now refers only to itself (p. 7; 15) and equally to 'politics, law and aesthetics' (p. 4; 12). Each domain has attempted to be all-encompassing, each driving itself into being its own simulacrum, and each then turns on itself, fractalizing. This is a moment of danger, as we have lost all illusion, and illusion is what has given us reality. So the first phase in the theory of impossible exchange is the closing off of exchange with death, illusion, Evil, and so on. The inhuman, too, must go: 'we are moving everywhere towards an elimination of the Inhuman, towards an anthropological integrism which aims to submit everything to the jurisdiction of the Human' (p. 16; 26). However, this is not a triumph of humanism, it is instead the end of it, as 'we deprive ourselves of any idea of the Human as such. For this can come to us only from the Inhuman' (ibid.).[10]

We are then at the point of impossible exchange, and law, economics or humanism have all to face up to the impossibility of external reference or grounding. At the point of success, of complete simulation, domains of activity and/or thought are brought to face up to their nothingness. So even if illusion or Evil are diminished, impossible exchange remains as an ultimate reality, a reality of Nothing: 'Death, illusion, absence, the negative, evil, the accursed share are everywhere, running beneath the surface of all exchanges. It is even this continuity of Nothing which grounds the possibility of the Great Game of Exchange' (p. 7 trans. mod.; 16).[11]

So the endpoint of simulation is the revelation or denial of impossible exchange, but it also intervenes within simulation and drives 'the fractal' that Baudrillard identified as a fourth stage of simulation (see *Transparency*, p. 5; 13), as the hyperrealized world turns from its only reality: 'all our systems are converging in a desperate effort to escape radical uncertainty, to conjure away the inevitable, fateful fact of impossible exchange. Commercial exchange, exchange of meaning, sexual exchange – everything has to be exchangeable' (*Impossible Exchange*, p. 14; 24). All exchange comes to be seen as valuable, all communication good in its own right. The word 'exchange' itself takes on a terminally positive value (as in 'cultural exchange') as it empties itself out of purpose beyond itself. While that occurs at a cultural, or even global, level, individuals, too, are faced with impossible exchange, and with no-one to exchange with, or perhaps to, as Baudrillard is thinking of God, or 'higher values' (p. 13; 23). Individuals turn in on themselves, demanding the right to 'be myself', which is the lowest form of right, of freedom (p. 52; 77). What does it mean to 'just be yourself'? According to Baudrillard, this is the end of the self, the point at which the subject is lost. Then, the individual becomes fractal (part of the mass – the individual as bearer of the mass, a unit of it at best) and viral, turned on itself. This viral self emerges from what we might think of as resistance to simulation, transparency, and so on. Baudrillard criticizes body art, extreme sports and drug-taking as just so many more experiments on the self, which is already being endlessly tested, surveyed, monitored (pp. 48–9; 68–9). While he is correct to see these as nostalgic (p. 48; 68), he is too quick to dismiss them entirely, given the high possibility that some of those performance artists, in particular, are highly aware they are not restoring some great lost body or spirituality. Even David Blaine's appropriation of the hunger strike as a publicity-driven endurance feat, a perfect simulation, is also a perfect example of the form such feats take in contemporary society. Furthermore, like Disneyland, David Blaine is there to enhance the authenticity of the rest, all of which is now simulated, nostalgic. At a more mundane, if equally banal, level, individuals turn impossible exchange inwards when they try to change themselves, to always 'be different'. Leaving aside the commercialization that drives such notions, Baudrillard argues that this takes the elimination of the self further. In demanding the 'right to be oneself', the content is removed, and the self being asked for is fractalized, ultimately empty (which returns us to something of a truth about all notions of the self). Finally, you cannot exchange your own life, as there is nowhere for it to go (pp. 77–8; 99–100).

Beyond the world of subjects lies the response of the object, or reality itself. As it gets consumed in knowledge and visibility, it starts to trick its observers, leaving passivity behind:

> A docile – if not, indeed, hyper-docile – reality bends to all hypotheses, and verifies them all without distinction. For reality, it is all merely a superficial and provisional 'enframing' [*Gestell*] in the Heideggerian sense. Reality itself has become simulative, and leaves us with a sense of its fundamental unintelligibility, which has nothing mystical about it, but would seem, rather, to be ironic. (p. 23; 35)

At this point there is nowhere for us to turn. Even the thing we imagine to be reality has no guarantee, cannot itself be guarantee, and it has the nerve to disrupt the simulacra we have constructed to keep illusion and the impossibility of exchange hidden. The only manoeuvre left is to go virtual. With the virtual, we have 'a fantastical general equivalent' (*Mots de passe*, p. 92). The virtual, constructed out of 'the alternance 0/1' approaches impossible exchange in being undecidable (p. 93), yet also fatal: the value will be either 0 or 1. Simulation tries to escape its limit in the virtual, the real tries to save itself in the virtual, but it is impossible exchange and nothingness that are further developed in the move.

Luckily for us, writes Baudrillard, illusion does not go away: illusion still brings appearances into being, and therefore brings the world, even if this illusion is also wrapped up in the real. Like all Baudrillard's concepts for what there is other than simulation in a simulated world, impossible exchange is far from being positive, and is nothing of a way out. The Good is always on the side of 'the system': only the ambiguous, in some ways the Evil, can bring us out to ourselves, to the world. Getting there will only return you to another 'falsity' (the choice is between a form of simulation or a form of illusion), and this could be a violent process, but, if nothing else, there seems to be a sense that knowing about it helps, and in some ways helps you, within the hyperreal world. This does not mean we can control it, for what all these dualistic forms suggest is a form of radical quietism, where events are allowed to occur (*Impossible Exchange*, pp. 61–2; 83).

Notes

1. There is a brief, and belated, attempt to claim a history for seduction and a historicization of the book, in the conclusion of *Seduction*. According to Baudrillard, we can follow Walter Benjamin's formulation of the changing status of art and apply this to seduction. Art is firstly of ritual, then aesthetic, and finally, political value. Seduction goes from highly formalized ritual (which does not imply predictability), to being a (differently) formalized aesthetic, and then ends up emptied, and political, complicit with simulation (for example, and possibly ironically, politics) (p. 180; 246).
2. We should balance this echo of Freud's statement that 'the sexual life of adult women is a "dark continent" for psychology' ('The Question of Lay Analysis', *Standard Edition*, 20, p. 212) with Baudrillard's statement that maybe the male is residual, responding to female power of reproduction, with

women more or less the only sex (pp. 15–16; 30–1). Although he doesn't pursue this, it is worth noting that this is the view genetic science has eventually come around to.

3. Baudrillard is unwittingly close to Hélène Cixous, in her analysis of Freud's 'Dora', ('Portrait of Dora', in *Benmussa Directs: Portrait of Dora and the Singular Life of Albert Nobbs*, pp. 27–67.

4. See Derrida, 'Cogito and the History of Madness', in *Writing and Difference*, pp. 31–63, in which Derrida criticizes Foucault for valorizing madness as an outside, rather than being the totally necessary Other, which is neither inside nor outside. See also Bataille, 'The Obelisk', in *Visions of Excess*, pp. 213–22. In this essay, Bataille argues that the solidity and durability of the monument (to the Revolution, in this case) constitute the specific embodiment of the threat of its non-existence. At a more mundane level, historical hindsight might also point to the imposition of 'Reason' through 'The Terror' as being the problem, rather than there being a necessary core of irrationality as the included outside of Reason.

5. In addition, there is the possibility of (an always vanished?) symbolic power which is in, and an acceptance of, an economy of loss, expenditure, death (pp. 54–5; 75). Seduction precedes and 'encourages' sexuality, while having an influence beyond seduction as it is more usually conceived, at a mundane level, as something within sex or desire. Seduction is only connected with sex by default. Seduction is primarily a form of symbolic violence.

6. This applies just as much to the scientific investigation of undecidability. As Gane observes, 'the analysis of radical uncertainty is only the examination of certain conditions of possibility' (*In Radical Uncertainty*, p. 56).

7. A similar case is made by Monique Wittig, attacking the valorizing of women's 'difference' (see *The Straight Mind*), and also by Flann O'Brien/Myles na gCopaleen, in *The Poor Mouth/An Béal Bocht* and elsewhere, when writing of what purports to be the preservation of a culture.

8. Why is agency a problem? It would imply that there is a way out of simulation, and therefore that it is not an all-encompassing system. At the very least, though, Baudrillard,

throughout his writings, suggests implicitly that knowing about simulation is possible.

9. These pages are unpaginated in the English version.

10. This echoes Giorgio Agamben in his reading of 'the Holocaust' and the ways in which it has been thought. See *Remnants of Auschwitz* and *Homo Sacer: Sovereign Power and Bare Life*.

11. As at many points in his œuvre, Baudrillard might seem nostalgic for a time when the real was real, as in the following statement: 'there is no "objective" reality any more. We may as well accept this, and stop dreaming of a situation that is long dead' (*Impossible Exchange*, p. 21; 33). Objective reality, and any other sort of reality, for that matter, are products of radical illusion, the indeterminacy of which allows appearances, allows the world to come to be and also not be, and certainly not to simply be as it appears (see pp. 9–10; 19).

Chapter 4

Geopolitics of the Real

The transpolitical world

The era of simulation, or hyperreality, brings serious changes in the world of politics and alters the nature of events (and this in turn feeds simulation). Now that, according to Baudrillard, nothing is genuinely real, we see an increased insistence on reality, on 'the political', and the social. Sincerity is valued as such, rather than as a means of delivering specific ideological goals, and, of course, when you hear the word sincerity, this does not mean genuine honesty. For someone who seeks not to be a critic, but a hyperbolic theorist of extremes, Baudrillard's writings betray a continual interest in politics, and often provide a critical perspective, even if it is not critique in the sense of exposing a hidden, ideological truth.

Politics has to leave its old terms behind, even itself. The political is over, and now we are in the 'transpolitical', where the old terms persist, but have no purchase on a genuine reality (see *In the Shadow*, p. 40; 44, and *Fatal Strategies*, p. 25; 29). The transpolitical is when politics is everywhere (and transparency is the ubiquitous appearance of a phenomenon, rather than that we clearly see, or see through something (*Fatal Strategies*, p. 44; 51)). At this point, the old referents no longer work, and we need to replace ideas such as the State, classes or ideologies, with terrorism, the event, the obese even (in which Baudrillard was briefly interested as one of the 'figures of the transpolitical' in *Fatal Strategies*). We also need to recast terms such as the social and the masses, as well as the notion of power itself.

Baudrillard's attempt to move beyond Foucault, *Forget Foucault*, was published in 1977, by which time Foucault was established as possibly the major thinker of the time, in France, at least, and anyone writing on politics, power or contemporary society would be more or less obliged to deal with his work (like Sartre before him). For Baudrillard, Foucault's thought of power (in *Discipline and Punish* and *The History of Sexuality*) is as far as we can go, and signals the limit of both power and the analysis of it. In completing the thought of power, writes Baudrillard, and claiming that power imbues everything in modern Western society (thereby effectively imprisoning all of us), Foucault has actually emptied power – not by removing any critical value it might have as a term, but in revealing that power ends itself (*Forget Foucault*, p. 33; 45). It does not weaken or dissipate, but leaves the real behind and becomes a simulation (p. 51; 69–71). Simulated power is no less oppressive (if we think power equals oppression), but cannot be fought (although terrorism offers a hint of a break in simulation). Dead power is like the dead God of Nietzsche: no-one seems to have realized that God is dead, but the burden of the corpse weighs heavier than the live God/live power (p. 59; 82). The most able politicians use this, and function specifically in the realm of dead power. An example of this, although Baudrillard seems to regard it as too obvious to even state, is the politician who realizes that what the voters are interested in are superficial qualities. The example he gives is much more counter-intuitive. He argues that fascism comes after the end of power (p. 61; 84). We might argue that Nazism, in particular, is the height of power, and that would really be the point: in becoming total, power under the Nazis is not *directed* the same way as before. It also appeals to the gap left in liberal democracies, in reactivating myths of origin, of belonging, ceremonies, the visualization of power.[1] Totalitarianism creates 'the social', to replace the society of the past, a simulation of what was supposedly there in the past, 'the violent reactivation of the social in a society that despairs of its own rational and contractual foundation' (p. 61; 84).

Perversely (or is it ironically?), it is the left, after World War II, that tries to create this lost 'social', in the form first of all of the expansion of the Welfare State, and then later to argue against the neo-liberal, right-wing notion that the individual is all that counts.

All positive thought about the social is complicit with the now hyperreal power of capital/liberal States: 'the social itself must be considered a model of simulation and a form to be overthrown since it is a strategic form of value brutally positioned by capital and then idealized by critical thought' (*Forget Foucault*, p. 53; 73). Capital inaugurated the social in the wake of the 1929 Stock Market crash and the ensuing Depression (*In the Shadow*, p. 27; 31). In order to function, consumerism had to be encouraged, and production would now operate in thrall to advertising or propaganda-led demand. To summarize, the social is a construct first of capitalism, then pushed further in totalitarianism, and then recuperated by the non-revolutionary left. By the 1980s, the social, like power, is everywhere, and therefore non-existent as an actual reality (pp. 18–19; 24). Society itself, as a concept and as a reality, is the victim of this success. Like an updated Bataille, Baudrillard suggests that other older societies had some sort of reality, and were in some way actually communal, in stating that the social is built on 'the ruins of the symbolic and ceremonial edifice of former societies' (p. 65; 69).

The social is itself ruin, a self-created one, as its interests lie in its own margins, which it probes and fosters at every stage. The social is aligned with all that has become residual: social issues are to do with ill-health, discrimination, exclusion, problematic behaviours (*In the Shadow*, p. 75; 79). We have even invented a new domain of production, in the form of social work. The social is precisely not a unified society or community, but a set of networks or circuits, each isolated from the other, and within which the social deals with you as an isolated individual (p. 83; 87). The new social is a total construct, and knows it is one: constructing its hyperreality from statistics, polls, computer models (p. 20; 25). Individuals are no longer members of the community, but a set of data, a category, or a type. Where Foucault wrote of the use of biopower (regulation of bodies and their movement), Baudrillard observes the next phase, where we are defined by information. As with Foucault, it seems that some are in a better position than others (e.g. shops compared to consumers), but power no longer cares about who it is controlling. That is the error in criticizing CCTV, for example, on the grounds of invasion of privacy: when we're all on TV, no-one will be any more interesting than anyone else. The protest is a desperate attempt to recreate a sense of counting for someone or something, but simulated power is the coldest (or coolest) of all. When a shop loyalty card processes information about your purchases, they are not interested in you, the process is interested in breaking you down, so that 'you' don't count, but your purchases (or 'choices') do.

The social is not inhabited by classes, but occupied by the masses, described by Baudrillard as 'a black hole which engulfs the social' (*In the Shadow*, p. 4; 9). The masses are created as a by-product of consumerism, and the mass society configured by nineteenth-century capitalism. Both governments and businesses loved the conformity and malleability of the masses, but this succeeded too well (p. 23; 28). Now power has to encourage people to join in (for example, in the form of voting, a pastime increasingly dismissed by the masses). The masses have become a form of inert resistance (p. 41; 46), incapable of taking the 'choices' offered by market capitalism or market democracy. Alternatively, the masses resist through 'hyperconformity' (p. 47; 52): for example, in following the latest health recommendations or scares (p. 46; 51), overloading email or phone lines when called on to participate in 'interactive' TV products, or accepting the fears inculcated by governments to the point of panic (as in America since September 2001).

Some might say that the media are at least partly responsible for the mass-ification of society, but for Baudrillard, they are part of the same phenomenon ('the mass and the media are one single process', *In the Shadow*, p. 44; 48), and, as noted above, in their massness, resist their own subjection (there is no possibility of alienation). So how is it that there is such a strong belief that the mass media manipulate the masses? It suits the TV channels or newspapers to believe that, and it also suits critics of the mass media, who keep the notion of unalienated agency alive (i.e. once the ideology of the media is revealed, the mass will realize they have been controlled and break free; the drawback is that even were such a thing possible, there would be no content for the emptied mass-individual to work with). However, Baudrillard can be criticized here for refusing to deal with the question of access to the media. Even if we accept his view entirely, it is still the case that some have greater access to transmission, and others are more likely to be passive receivers (and none more passive than one who is drawn into 'interaction'). So some messages are more likely to be heard than others, and some will benefit financially from this. As a counter-argument, we might note the democratization of media access through the Internet and cheaper, readier access to it, but this is restricted to certain areas of the world, and as 'the' Internet is global, only the names of the monopolizers have changed.

The masses, for their part, are happy for power to be taken from them, exercised for them. The masses thereby change the nature of power, deadening it and paradoxically reducing its hold on the real world, or what is thought of as such. The masses are not necessarily the same as the lower classes of a society: they are a phenomenon created as part of the change from an era of production (which did have clearly defined lower classes) to one of simulation. They might be lumpen, but they're not proletariat. As individuals they no longer suffer the anomie of the dispossessed. Instead they tend to the anomalous (*Fatal Strategies*, p. 25; 29): they don't fit into society, but they don't care; crime is increasingly inefficient and aimless; the system continually tries to place them and fails. The ultimate endpoint of this is terrorism.

Terrorism

It might seem odd to think of terrorism as a product of simulated society, but that is how Baudrillard has consistently seen it since the mid-1970s. Terrorism resists the certainties of an atrophied power system, and attacks the system (a State, or the global 'system'), not an ideology as such. For Baudrillard, terrorism is not about the supposed goals of an organization, but a process that exceeds these goals while using them as its initial rationale.

Simulation itself is terroristic, with 'terrorism . . . always that of the real' (*Simulacra*, p. 47; 75), as it imposes itself arbitrarily and tries to affect each individual as part of a subjected mass. 'Terrorism responds by an *equally hyperreal* act, caught up from the outset in concentric waves of media and fascination' (*In the Shadow*, p. 50; 55), in other words, there would be no terrorism without the masses and the mass media, or a world where power has become its own simulation. Terrorism is both of the system and its opposite (see *In the Shadow*, p. 113; *Le Ludique et le policier*, p. 429).[2] It is neither simply evil, nor merely simulation, but evil as simulation (*Transparency*, p. 81; 88).

In terms of the practice of terror as a strategy (and not as an ideological description of the opposing forces in an armed struggle), Baudrillard emphasizes the relevance of arbitrariness rather than rational selection. This arbitrariness attacks the system's undifferentiation, the fact that all individuals are substitutable. Not only are the masses all targets, they are also targeted through the media, first, in terms of spreading fear, second, in submitting to the media's fascination for violence. In these terms, the media's encouragement of the fear of child abduction could also be described as terrorism. This is not, in Baudrillard's view, a fear generated by the media in order to sell its product: the masses are part of this phenomenon, and conspire in their own fearful fascination.

Terrorism exceeds the intention of the terrorist, especially if it is political. For Baudrillard, terrorism is something that imbues all latter-day simulation, and 'the terrorist act is akin to the natural catastrophe' (*In the Shadow*, p. 56; 61), although this catastrophe could also be something brought about by humanity, such as the failure of a nuclear reactor. So when we look at terrorism that ostensibly targets a policy, a nation, a race, Baudrillard claims we are missing the reality of the *terrorism* involved, and misreading it as guerrilla warfare: 'Do the Palestinians strike at Israel by means of intermediary hostages? No, it is through Israel as intermediary that they strike at a mythical, or not even mythical, anonymous, undifferentiated enemy' (*In the Shadow*, p. 55; 60). Baudrillard knows that that is not how it is perceived by those most directly involved, but he wants to look at how terrorism functions as a category, rather than using it as an accusatory description, and if you add the words 'such as the West' to the end of the last quote, it already seems more feasible.

The 1970s were the first era where terrorism could be enacted on a global scale, thanks not only to the news media, but also transport media, principally the growth of air travel. Many 'terrorist groups' were most active in this period, whether fighting for national sovereignty, independence, a revolution, or simply to get prisoners released. The hostage was a key bargaining chip. For

Baudrillard, though, this activity is far from being the end of terrorism, as States also began to act in the same way, with the superpowers holding populations to ransom, and ultimately the whole world, due to the threat of nuclear war (one element that is very much of its time in Baudrillard's writings on simulation is the insistence on deterrence, which has faded in the 'real' world since the fall of the Soviet Union in 1989). States are also called on to respond to terrorism, and this requires actions beyond the law, and beyond the usual rules of military engagement: i.e. terrorism (*In the Shadow*, pp. 115–16; *Le Ludique et le policier*, pp. 432–3). Counter-terrorism is part of what it claims to be fighting (the Spanish State's 'death squads' working against the Basque separatists, ETA; the British State's approach to the IRA; Israel's attacks on Hamas leaders, even during ceasefires; the USA's 'war on terrorism' that emerged after 9/11).[3] When this occurs, terrorism has won, as it has brought reversibility into the system (p. 116; 433), and is also able to claim that it has exposed the true violence of the system (like the anarchist 'propaganda by the deed' of the early twentieth century).

Whether we agree with Baudrillard or not about the politicized forms of terrorism, we could add evidence to support his general point, when we think of the spread of terror as weapon, against, for example, 'minorities', refugees, even categories of employee (such as civil servants). Individuals have taken terrorism for themselves. There are those in the USA who believe the State is betraying them by restricting their freedom, there are those throughout the world who take a personal grudge and punish arbitrarily. Mass killers, particularly when they are 'ordinary' children, are a perfect example of terror being 'anomalous' rather than 'anomic' (*Fatal Strategies*, p. 34; 39), and it would be a mistake to think of events such as the Columbine murders as manifestations of alienation. They are the spectacle of alienation, its simulation, and are much more like part of a machine going random. This sounds a little like the argument put up by those who blame TV and music for violence, so it is worth clarifying that cause and effect are absolutely lost in terrorism. If there is a link, maybe it is one caused by the world of simulation (previously the real world), where the real is pursued so vigorously. Maybe it's a protest against those who would fictionalize, mythologize and romanticize violence.

War

Very early on, Baudrillard wrote of wars not happening, as they were subsumed into media representations, models of what would occur, and a global model of deterrence, which meant that the real war (USA v. Soviet Union) could not happen. As noted above (Chapter 2), the fact that wars are simulated actually makes them more dangerous for anyone caught up in them (suggesting a residual reality in the form of those being attacked), and makes some wars a combat of reality against simulation (in the case of the first Gulf War, the coalition fighting Iraq expected something like a real war, and Iraq played a different game; in Yugoslavia, America believed war had fully entered simulation, but the Serbs dragged war back into the real).

The theory of the non-occurrence of real war is completed in Baudrillard's controversial thoughts on the unreality of the first Gulf War. If the Vietnam War was the first media war, and therefore a shift in what war was to be, the first Gulf War against Iraq (1991) was the same but more so.[4] It was the first war to need to be justified as real (a similar thing is occurring in the aftermath of Gulf War 2, where the drive to justify is relentless).

Baudrillard wrote a series of pieces before, during and after the first Gulf War, arguing, respectively, that it would not take place, was not taking place, and did not take place. These were rapidly collected as *The Gulf War Did Not Take Place*, a book robustly criticized, in the absence of a close reading, by Christopher Norris, in *Uncritical Theory*.[5] The primary reason Baudrillard gives for the non-occurrence of the war is its pre-emption in media. This has two elements: first, the public or mass media rendering the war into a simulacrum of itself, and of war in general (this particularly through the 'real-time' coverage), and second, through the military's own use of new media, in the form of information technology. The combination of these prevents real war occurring, because it has always already taken place (*The Gulf War*, pp. 35–6; 27–8).[6] Unlike Noam Chomsky, Baudrillard sees no mystification or ideological control by or through the media. The media have a range of uncontrollable effects, many of which might decrease political legitimation of war, not least because it becomes entertainment, and loses the distinction between true and false (thus the popularity of 'Comical Ali' in Gulf War 2 hinged on his disregard for truth to the extent that he was not really lying).

Military use of new technology undermines the need for the actual war to take place. Not only does it mean war does not need to happen, it ensures it never can by ironizing its own technological level, in the form of disastrously inaccurate 'surgical strikes', or death by 'friendly fire'. Baudrillard writes elsewhere that 'all our technologies might, therefore, be said to be the instrument of a world we believe we rule, whereas in fact the world is using this machinery to impose itself, and we are merely spectators' (*The Perfect Crime*, p. 71; 106). Superficially, though, Baudrillard is utterly wrong about this: a war, or something very similar, did take place, and resulted in the loss of much Iraqi life. As we know, however, the simulatedness of a war makes it even more dangerous, as it is being fought for no reason, and seems to wish to counter the predictions (in this case, the obsession with a 'clean' war, leading to 'simulated losses' (*The Gulf War*, p. 44; 41)).[7] As well as this, the Gulf War is about selling hardware and American intervention as a service (p. 30; 20), and also the apparent democracy of blanket TV coverage accessible all around the world (CNN taking over from the British World Service).

So the US-led coalition could claim a multiple victory: militarily, politically, with the construction of a coalition itself, and economically. All of these are within the realm of simulation, however, as Saddam Hussein also wins, by not being defeated, by opposing the USA in the first place, and, despite running an essentially secular regime, and having fought Iran, and Iraq's Shia population, acquiring Muslim support. In other words, the military 'reality' is one of the least significant components of what did happen. Baudrillard claims that Saddam was able to use the media much better than the coalition against Iraq, and this is not due to his control of media, but his use of spectacle (for example, of prisoners (p. 39; 33), or human shields), raising the possibility that excessive simulation gets you beyond the simulated world's insistence on its own reality.

The conduct of the war also contributes to its not happening: this is the war that insisted on 'surgical strikes', which were less accurate than the bombings of World War II, and in fact means we don't know what is left, or actually hit, because the enemy's communications are down, and 'we' stay at a distance, unable to tell how many rocket launchers are left (p. 43; 39), or indeed chemical weapons. This lack of direct encounters (except with retreating troops) meant that the modelling of the war took precedence, and also that total belief in computerized defence systems caused 'friendly fire' casualties. It also meant that the USA never fought the Other, unable to imagine it as anything other than another me (pp. 37, 39; 30, 34), and would never defeat that Other. This situation is still (not) occurring with the 'war against terrorism'. That war, like the Gulf War, will not end, even with Saddam's capture, because it never really started, or happened, or as Baudrillard put its, 'since it never began, this war is therefore interminable' (p. 26; 14).

In the 'real' world, the war was unceasing, apparently causing more deaths through the ensuing sanctions than the number killed in the war. Saddam also continued to attack 'his own people', and this went unpunished, just as it had been ignored while Iraq fought Iran in the 1980s, and the West armed Saddam. The West, notably the USA and Britain, has used this 'internal violence' as justification for its recent war on Iraq. Does this show cynicism? Of course, but it also shows the total contempt for truth and falsity: this blatant rewriting of history is all the legitimation that seems to be required, so why provide more? When the USA and Britain did provide more, it was as comical as anything produced on the other side, with a dated, plagiarized thesis, invented purchases of material for weapons, imagined links to al-Qaida, and a clearly paranoid faith in the strength of Saddam and the efficiency of his military. Baudrillard's argument has been superseded by actual events, as the US/British coalition had to claim that these weapons of mass destruction were dismantled just before the invasion, rather than being used against the enemy and possibly saving the regime, and this came after the initial claim that not having the weapons was not enough, as proof was needed they had been destroyed. Finally, if everyone won the first war, I think we could say everyone lost this one, and, needless to say, it too will not end.

There was one winner: not al-Qaida or Osama bin Laden, but

al-Jazeera, which took over from the Western cable channels as the station of reference. The USA and Britain came up with a novel idea for controlling the news, which was to 'embed' journalists, and vet their reports. While journalists who stayed in Baghdad ritually mentioned their 'reporting restrictions', the 'embedded' journalist would maintain the realness of their report, benefitting media and military alike, until outflanked by a surprisingly objective al-Jazeera (given its previous reputation as the site for transmitting messages from bin Laden), which is not to say they were truer, but that they matched the criteria for attributing truth within the media, and dwelt on the spectacle of death, drawing it into simulation in a way the Western channels could (or would) not. In many ways, Western reporting went back to before the Vietnam War, and fell back on a nostalgic mode where the inability to tell all offers a guarantee of the seriousness both of the situation and the media's responsible attitude, while being in the thick of events.

Equally nostalgic has been the decade of violence in what used to be Yugoslavia, with its insistence on mass killing, and the literalism of ethnic cleansing. Baudrillard is highly cynical about the Western European perception of what has occurred there, and suggests that the West is desperate for reality, and its criteria for that are suffering, war and death. It only has the 'lowest common denominator' of feeling for the plight of the victims (*The Perfect Crime*, pp. 134–5; 186), for what gets called 'human tragedy'. He also makes a very interesting statement about the reality of war, in saying that 'the real' might well be making a reappearance here, but only for those inflicted by it (p. 133; 184), and even this reality is diminished (or heightened into hyperreality) through the presence of the media. The real, then, is being made to submit to violence: not for the first time, Baudrillard is suggesting that simulation actually has a useful function, keeping violence away (although in the long run, like overdoing antibiotic use, this leads to new vulnerability).[8]

Baudrillard also writes on the massacre at Timisoara, which it would later turn out was not one, and the centrality of the media in the dismantling of the old Romanian regime, with the control and use of TV a major part of it (*Illusion*, p. 56; 86). Everywhere he looks, it seems, a war has some element that removes truth from it – at least for us in the West, believing we see all that happens, with the moral exhortation to 'know what's going on in the world', coming at us from all ideological perspectives. In light of Baudrillard's profound scepticism, we need also to look at what he says about the Holocaust. As with Lyotard, it is not enough to say that holocaust deniers/*négationnistes* are wrong (which he says anyway, see *Screened Out*, p. 108; 122): you also need to emphasize that the grounds on which they make their argument – lack of evidence and doubt – disqualify them from claiming the Holocaust did occur, and means that attempts to scientifically assess gas residues, etc., runs counter to their aim. Non-deniers need also to be aware that to commemorate the mass murder of millions of Jews is also a diminution of it, as it transforms what occurred into hyperreal, mediatized 'reality', reducing the real event, while at the same time, replaying it, re-enacting it, to some extent (referring specifically to *Shoah*, and *Holocaust*, in *Transparency of Evil*, p. 91; 97: the book's title echoes Hannah Arendt's *Eichmann in Jerusalem: A Report on the Banality of Evil*). The denial of the Holocaust is bizarre, because there is so much proof of it occurring (even though Auschwitz itself has largely had to be rebuilt), so for Baudrillard, this is perhaps the most important thing to watch out for: it's not the absence of proof, or 'moral relativism' that lets the Nazis back in. Today the excess of truth, the hyperrealization of everything, means that no event, however momentous and violent, can elude simulation. This is the danger (*Transparency*, pp. 91–3; 97–9).

The end of the event

Many would accept that a combination of a global economy based on speculation and pure (i.e. non-referential) value, globalized mass media, the gradual disappearance of any ideology opposed to capitalism and the sanitization of Western life adds up to something like simulation. The prime exception, though, would be war, which for Baudrillard is not only part of an increasingly virtual world, but a cause of that virtualization. The last possibility, then, is an event which would interrupt the flow of a controlled human ecosystem. How would this event strike us? Essentially, our access to the event is through the media, and, above all, real-time TV.

This, though, is precisely where we encounter the non-event, as real-time coverage is only 'the spectacle of the degradation of the event' (*The Gulf War*, p. 48; 47). This is because real-time captures the event, and accounts for it, processing it so it cannot be a brutal irruption – it is always only a virtual event: 'the closer we approach the real time of the event, the more we fall into the illusion of the virtual' (p. 49; 48). Real-time TV is not the arrival of a perpetual uncritical present, as Paul Virilio writes in *Desert Screen*, but of a perpetually absent, withheld, commented, pre-empted present that becomes uninhabitable.[9]

Events still hold Baudrillard's attention, and take precedence over static or enduring situations, hence his interest in writing for the newspaper *Libération*, which also allows a speedy response to what is occurring. This is because in some way we are in the end of ideology, and/or the end of history predicted by Daniel Bell, Raymond Aron, Alexandre Kojève and Francis Fukuyama. Baudrillard does not accept the capitalist-triumphalist model for this. If Margaret Thatcher thought she saw the writing on the wall for communism before 1989, then she is in the interesting company of Marx, who most of one and a half centuries earlier was aware that communism, in, for example, Russia, without the leading economic powers also being communist, would be doomed. Baudrillard instead refers to Elias Canetti's notion of a history that has ended without anyone noticing (*Illusion*, p. 1; 11, but referred to by Baudrillard in the much earlier *À l'Ombre des majorités silencieuses*, p. 95).[10] In this model, we carry on as if history were not over, and it can never end because it has always already ended. The fabled end of history is only an illusion, and even specific, anticipated events, such as 'the millennium' of 2000, will not occur (*Illusion*, p. 9; 22) and the threatened 'millennium bug' did not take place.

History is over, then, while being unable to finish (*Illusion*, p. 4; 15 and *passim*). This is caused by the meaninglessness of what occurs once we have a simulated world. Baudrillard concurs with 'end of history' thinkers to the extent that the linear march of History towards a specific endpoint is over, but their model always implies a triumph for a particular ideology, and that therefore we actually have arrived 'somewhere'. Baudrillard's model, though, is based on the dispersal of the linear, and the located:

Every political, historical and cultural fact possesses a kinetic energy which wrenches it from its own space and propels it into a hyperspace where, since it will never return, it loses all meaning . . . Now, through the impulse for total dissemination and circulation, every event is granted its own liberation; . . . No event can stand being beamed across the whole planet. No meaning can withstand acceleration. (p. 2; 12)

There is a crucial shift in the status of the event, which occurs within the time of its 'liberation', such that as it comes to mean, it loses meaning. Clearly this has something to do with the mass-mediatized world, but as with everything in, during and arguably after simulation, cause and effect is lost. In this case, historical events themselves also undo history as narrative. Baudrillard writes of the clock being turned back, with the end of the Cold War, and the reinvention of nation-states, their myths and their bloody con-flicts (pp. 11, 32; 25, 54).

The media and masses are central to the process of non-ending, though, and in the event becoming non-event. In contemporary society, events only count if mediatized (pp. 15–16; 30–1). Once mediatized, especially if through 'real-time', the event loses its sit-uatedness in historical narrative, and loses its singularity as these are replaced by commentary, and the modelling of events (the decisions as to what constitutes an event, how to show it, who to ask about it, what 'the public' wishes to see and what background is to be supplied). Things did occur, Baudrillard claims, but no longer, as 'in earlier times an event was something that happened – now it is something that is designed to happen. It occurs, there-fore, as a virtual artefact' (*Transparency*, p. 41; 48). As events break free, memory of them becomes impossible (yet encouraged, just as the real is in simulation, with the 'experience' you had of the event, in the form of 'where were you when . . .'), linearity is therefore undone, and meaningfulness (i.e. reality) disappears. The irony is that 'the event' was reality's last chance – the last pockets of the real unfolding in real-time. Instead, events become 'black holes' (*Illusion*, p. 20; 36).[11]

Real-time events are virtual, not real, as the real is replaced (*The Vital Illusion*, p. 50), and when an event occurs, the site is virtualized (*Illusion*, p. 56; 85). It also comes to precede the normally simulated world (*Paroxysm*, p. 30; 60). The virtual can be seen in a different light within a global theory of simulation: first, an extension, a new (non-)dimension of hyperreality, even its perfection; second, it is something beyond the progression of simulacra, as it is a willed, perfect copy – a conscious replacement of reality rather than its desperate assertion (hence the claim that the virtual undoes the 'society of the spectacle' (*Screened Out*, p. 153; 171); third, it is some form of resistance to reality/simulation. Baudrillard has suggested that virtual events protect us from actual ones (the Gulf War, the virtual crash of 1987).[12]

The virtual is the world of the non-event. Non-events can be events devoid of the serious intent of earlier versions, such as the 1995 strike in France, compared (nostalgically) to the revolutionary potential of May 1968 (*Screened Out*, pp. 126–7; 142–3). Much of what is in the news is a non-event (he cites paedophiles, unemployment and mad cow disease as examples of non-events (*Cool Memories IV*, p. 42; 57)). So the banal sense of a non-event, as simply an event that does not live up to expectations, or its predecessors, is in there, but this is secondary to the mediatization and massification of an event removing any force it would have had. The non-event is the way things occur and is exactly where we should look, although Baudrillard has problems if he is too close to what does (not?) occur, as with the recurrence of a second Gulf War, still not happening, only less so. To look at these events critically, however, is impossible. So while the death of Princess Diana is an example of a (Baudrillardian) non-event (*Impossible Exchange*, p. 137; 173), the point of interest has to be in its non-eventness, rather than analysing the media's culpability, or trying to get at what really happened.

Television is not the only screen, though. Although surprisingly Baudrillard only occasionally turns his attention to IT media, what he writes is of use when looking at the phenomenon. He notes that everything is now on line, and nothing can counter an on-line event (*D'un fragment*, p. 76). The on-line event unfolds in non-space, and theoretically in real-time, but its proximity to techniques of virtuality (television is a simulation technique trying to adapt to the virtual) means we are freed from imagining (hoping?) an event actually happened. The virtual consistently shows some signs of freedom, but it is an objective freedom, i.e. no *subject* will be freed in the virtual world. Anyone who believes that changing identity in chat rooms or old school multi-user environments is radical is caught in a model where identity matters, where the play can be ended and real subjectivity brought back (like Freud's Little Hans). The virtual might free people radically – free to live immense periods of time, or free to play games and dream forever. Alternatively, the virtual might remove the need for a body, extend the body, or our space might expand to include the virtual. This is all very interesting, but belongs to the techno-futurism of the 1960s and/or the 1980s. The virtual itself is a non-event, as we go recursively into a 1980s future mapped out by William Gibson, Bruce Sterling and Pat Cadigan. That's when we are not in the 1960s futures of Philip K. Dick or Marshall McLuhan.

9/11

Baudrillard writes that New York is the centre of the world (*America*, pp. 14–16; 20–1), because it is the only city wherein the development of capitalism is made manifest in its buildings, in its design (*Symbolic Exchange and Death*, p. 69; 108). Today, then, it the centre of a simulated, or possibly virtual world, where ideologies of the market, of individual freedom, of progress and the globalization that is most obvious in the omnipresence of certain (branded) products and media, emanate into and from that centre. This, in turn, is crystallized in the World Trade Center. In 1976, Baudrillard argued that this building real-ized the ultimate monopoly as being dual, bipolar (like DNA). The existence of two near-monopolies or even an oligopoly in the market ensures the continued domination of that group, with the semblance of competition. The twin towers are the perfect monopoly, as they do not merge in with the rest of the Manhattan skyline, and their doubling '*signifies* the end of all competition, the end of every original reference' (*Symbolic Exchange*, p. 69; 108). The fact that the towers are always already doubled (by each other) ends the representational space where we can distinguish original from copy. The World Trade Center becomes another moment in the passage to the simulation, and ultimately

the virtual world of globalization, and not just at the level of signifying, or illustrating, but at the level of hyper-realizing, as Baudrillard notes in dialogue with the architect Jean Nouvel (responsible for the four towers of the Bibliothèque Nationale in Paris). In this dialogue, he states that the World Trade Center 'expresses, signifies and translates, in a kind of full, constructed form, the context of a society already experiencing hyperreality' (*The Singular Objects of Architecture*, p. 4; 14). As we know, the hyperreality that is the globalizing West faces problems brought on by its monolithic nature – it begins to undermine itself, to behave anomalously and to encourage anomalies – perhaps the reason Baudrillard says New York is a 'catastrophic epicentre' (*Cool Memories IV*, p. 9 trans. mod.; 18). The destruction of the twin towers, is, in his view, the system attempting to destroy itself, or, at the very least, providing the conditions for this destruction.

Baudrillard's controversial reading of what is now known as 9/11 centres on this will to destruction generated by an all-powerful system, and refuses to attribute importance to any other motivation, or to a rationale of any sort. The event itself is an effect not only of relations between the USA and the world, or the Islamic world, or those who would resist globalization, but also of the virtualization of the world. Is the attack an irruption of some long-lost reality? Maybe, says Baudrillard, but that is not its importance. This lies in it combining the 'strategies' that counter simulation with simulation itself. This is what makes it a true event, one with world-wide significance because it is about globalization (*The Spirit of Terrorism*, p. 3; 9), and what makes it accessible to the world – the media, and its 'real-time' – is, moreover, what removes it from simply being real. Such an attack is the return of the global as violence: terroristic, mediatized, and capable of coming from anywhere.

The attack brings death back into a world that pretends it is not there, as the suicides of the pilots create more death, 'a death which is far more than real: a death which is symbolic and sacrificial' (p. 17; 25). The death of so many, so visibly, makes the event oscillate between real and its other (all it would exclude), and ultimately, what makes the event (not the act, or its direct consequences) symbolic is that it is an unreturnable challenge, an impossible exchange (*Power Inferno*, p. 30).[13] So far, this is a logical extension of earlier writings, but it is what he says about the West's role in the attack that moves it to another level of difficulty for some.

Baudrillard claims that 'we' (presumably the West) cannot totally dismiss an element of pleasure in the destruction of something at the heart of today's world system, the centre of world trade, by its own admission (*Spirit of Terrorism*, p. 4; 10). This is not anti-Americanism, because 'we' includes everyone, and it is our world that is being attacked. The USA has been looking for a symbolic wound, and it finally has one, allowing it to use the event as a sort of 'credit card' to do what it likes (*Power Inferno*, p. 40).[14] So, the first point about the destruction is that 'we' wanted it. The second is that the towers themselves commit suicide, in collapsing, thus offering some sort of response, on the part of the system, to the attack (the only thing to have the measure of suicide as a gift of death is to return your own death (*Spirit*, p. 7; 13)). We should not see this as personification of buildings, but as an indication that all the deaths and suicides here were effects of a system. Third, and more intuitively reasonable, is the argument that 'we' provided the attackers with everything they needed: the bulk of the terrorists involved were from one of the USA's major allies, Saudi Arabia, the pilots were trained in the USA, the planes were American and civilian, and the media provided the key element in making the attack a world-wide phenomenon. This complicity has its height in the various conspiracy theories spawned by the event, but an insistence on these would be, paradoxically, to rein in the impact of the attack, rationalizing it, and perhaps finally dismissing the 'opponent' (*Power Inferno*, p. 32).

Baudrillard himself is happy to dismiss the influence of ideology, correctly criticizing the insistence on martyrdom (*Spirit*, pp. 23–4; 33), but hasty in insisting that ideology has no part, either in the attacks, what the attackers might have been fighting against, or in the US response.[15] In terms of actual politics, though, he is clear – the violence of 9/11 has a reversibility which produces violence and counter-violence, as the USA 'tries to make the world secure'. Ultimately, the West now has an alibi to destroy those pockets of the world untamed by globalization, and spread undifferentiation (*Power Inferno*, pp. 75–6), while providing a 'police-state globalization' (*Spirit*, p. 32; 43).

It is easy to see how such an argument could provoke offence, or even derision, as those who insist on the reality of things love to cite violence as their evidence. The purpose of his provocation, though, is to try to force us out of our complacent humanism, and get us to approach that which we cannot understand: death, and the willingness to commit suicide to bring death. Without such a limit on our thinking, the attack on the World Trade Center would not have had anything like the same *type* of resonance, even if it still would have spurred calls for revenge. What is unthinkable in this event is not the loss of life (hence the simple lack of thought about massacres around the world in recent times), but the use of death in a staged exchange where a whole culture or world could be attacked. This event brings together many of the phenomena particular to simulation, meshed together with that which would be outside it. It also brings Baudrillard's thought to another peak of condensation, where it is precisely in how these thoughts are problematic that these articles are *philosophically* radical.

Notes

1. In this Baudrillard echoes Bataille, writing in the early 1930s, about the strength of Nazism being based on Western society's rejection of the sacred, and of non-rational phenomena. He further argued that the only way to combat Nazism would be to reactivate an opposing 'irrationality', as rational politics was outdone by the excessive character of Nazism (see 'The Psychological Structure of Fascism', *Visions of Excess*, pp. 137–60).

2. The translation of *À l'Ombre des majorités silencieuses* includes an additional essay 'Our Theatre of Cruelty' (*In the Shadow*, pp. 113–23) which is anthologized in *Le Ludique et le policier*, pp. 429–41.

3. The fact that these are all democracies is significant, as these claim to be popular non-violent regimes. It is not repression or State violence that is at stake here, or the list would be endless, but the moments where a system becomes what it is not supposed to be, i.e. its own enemy.

4. McLuhan and Fiore argue that with Vietnam, 'we are in the

midst of our first television war' (*War and Peace in the Global Village*, p. 134), and, furthermore, that 'every new technology necessitates a new war' (p. 98).

5. Baudrillard's book is thus unironically caught up in the world of simulation, of hyper-representation and mediatization that he seeks to expose.

6. Even before this, this version of war had occurred in J.G. Ballard's 'Secret History of World War 3', *War Fever*, pp. 23–32. Baudrillard refers to this text in *Fragments* (pp. 75–6; 86), and it is worth noting that Ballard is highly influential in Baudrillard's theory of simulation.

7. One way in which the war was 'safe' is that there were less deaths in road accidents, in many Western countries, while the war was on (*The Gulf War*, p. 74; 88).

8. The violence of the wars in what used to be Yugoslavia can be seen as a resistance to simulation (*Paroxysm*, pp. 17–18; 38).

9. Baudrillard and Virilio converge on many points regarding technology's determining of reality (and not just representations of it). For a comprehensive account of the subtle differences between them, see Gane, *In Radical Uncertainty*, pp. 77–87).

10. The essay 'L'extase du socialisme', in *À l'Ombre*, pp. 95–115, does not appear in *In the Shadow*.

11. Baudrillard is a bit confused here about which phenomenon is the black hole, as elsewhere he writes of nothing more happening because we cannot escape the 'event horizon' (i.e. the border of a black hole beyond which light does not escape), so reality would be the black hole beyond which events cannot escape – possibly a more satisfactory use of the idea (*Illusion*, p. 103; 145).

12. For Baudrillard, as the global economy is based on speculation and 'pure' value, the last possible real crash was 1929. We can only have virtual crashes now (see *Screened Out*, pp. 21–5; 31–5). Ultimately, however, the success of the virtual will mean our losing our status as spectators, witnesses, victims of surveillance, as the virtual environment will be total, and approach what McLuhan identified prematurely, perhaps, as the tactile world where all is in contact (and unable not to be) (see

McLuhan and Fiore, *War and Peace*, p. 163). Many presume the 'postmodern' surface world is only about images and the visual, but Baudrillard, like McLuhan, is describing a world where the visual has subsumed everything and in turn been subsumed, like power in Foucault.

13. The USA believes its 'war on terrorism' is just such a response, particularly in the form of its attacks on Afghanistan. Baudrillard characterizes such a response as a non-event, an incapacity to match the stakes set up by the attack on the World Trade Center (*Spirit*, p. 34; 45–6).

14. This occurs in many disaster films – maybe the withholding of certain films and music videos was not censorship or sympathy for victims, but acknowledgement they were no longer needed, according to this logic.

15. It cannot even be assessed in terms of the dispossessed versus the rich, as the problem should be seen in terms of the West's unreturnable gift of itself, responded to by another 'unreturnable' gift (*Power Inferno*, p. 79).

Chapter 5

Objects of Culture

Baudrillard has always been interested in a wide array of contemporary cultural phenomena, whether these are events, physical objects, developments in art or science, or the way in which the 'macro' world of simulation (and, increasingly, the virtual) permeates all within it, down to the 'micro' level. Baudrillard's take on the contemporary world could therefore be seen as synecdochal (the part is in the whole and vice versa), but for the fact that the possibility of distinction (as with map and territory) is gone, so we cannot talk about layers of representation. The part is the whole is the part. This applies horizontally, as well, in terms of how highly diverse events, institutions, theories and objects coalesce in his analyses. This chapter looks at a series of objects (in the broad sense) which generate resistances, even though many might presume these phenomena to be resistant in themselves.

System already follows this path in a structuralist fashion, taking objects such as furniture, clocks or cars not as examples, but as locations of the theory, and then considers the idea of 'ambience' that unites and homogenizes the domesticated modern world. This book already purposely strays from a consideration of high culture, but maintains a traditional sociological perspective insofar as an analysis of the collected parts will reveal a truth about the whole. Later on, but as early as *Symbolic Exchange*, analysis gives way to a sort of ironic repetition of how something like graffiti, the World Trade Center or striptease are the world they illustrate, no longer revealing anything about that world. His *Cool Memories* series floats assertively from assessments about travel to thoughts on particular city streets, or political developments, news events, space, celebrities, mad cows, medicine, and on and on. The style tells us about the superficiality of the world on show, but without a critical distance (there is criticism though), as these 'memories' are soundbite vacuous rather than aphoristically profound. Perhaps that in itself is a sort of critique (as in Bret Easton Ellis's *Glamorama*), but I think we might be closer to the spirit of them if we take them as fatally caught within simulation, and signalling the end (an end) of theory (that can never just stop).

In between the extremes of detailed structuralism and the fast theorizing of *Cool Memories* lies a range of obsessions that have been addressed in some detail by Baudrillard, and what is notable about these is that they are resolutely contemporary, and their newness drives at least some part of his own approach. In this, Baudrillard differs from the bulk of his French theoretical peers, who, for the most part, prefer to deal with new phenomena by placing them in a long history that has always already preceded what occurs now. Nor is it a given in France that the distinction between low and high culture has been disturbed as it is in Baudrillard. Baudrillard, of course, is not going to praise popular culture (except polemically), or valorize it as 'postmodern' media studies might, as it is just as caught up within simulated cultural reproduction as any other form of culture. He does have time, however, for the culture many might see as inflicted on the masses. The prime example is arguably reality TV, and as with many things (including cloning), Baudrillard was already dealing with this in the 1970s (*Simulacra and Simulation*, pp. 27–32; 48–56). Reality TV is of course nothing of the sort, as the presence of cameras distorts the reality, and, as early 2000s shows have shown, reality is too dull, so needs spicing up with adventurous tasks. As a result, the medium prevents the real from ever occurring (*The Perfect Crime*, p. 29; 50). Baudrillard also wrote that Disneyland was there to disguise the unreality of the rest of the USA (*Simulacra and Simulation*, p. 12; 26), and we might say the same about reality TV – its 'falsity' provides a convenient alibi for the supposed non-falsity of 'real life'. It is actually the search for authenticity that should bother us, in its hyperreality.

We are all involved (at least potentially) in reality TV (*Télémorphose*, p. 10), in the form of the 'participation' of the masses in mediatizing the world through camcorders, mobile, image and videophones, and CCTV.[1] Reality itself has become screen, and this is complete or total reality ('la réalité intégrale') (*Télémorphose*, p. 48). Baudrillard singles out the most successful reality TV show in France, *Loft Story*, and refers also to *Big Brother*. Both enclose the participants, establishing an experimental space of confinement, where ordinary behaviour can be studied (*Télémorphose*, p. 9). Despite these shows attempting to dramatize the situation, it is the banality that is interesting for the public (p. 11), and also the real object of the programme, as banality itself, and existence reduced to its realness, have so far eluded control, as they are the passive resistance of the masses. The omnipresence of cameras and screens in the 'real world' has encouraged people to participate in these TV non-events, and programmes have managed to incorporate the selection process, in the programmes that aim to create pop stars, or in an impoverishment of the truly banalized Japanese singer/personality 'idols', characters laughably called 'pop idols'. The term is truer than intended, and indicates that the visible element is what counts, so those who bemoan the lack of musical integrity have missed the point. Beyond 'reality TV', though, we, as the masses, both wish to be seen and not seen (p. 13): we want to appear, but not lose our 'privacy' (itself a highly mediatized concept). Cameras do not always want our image, either. Take the example of a sports event, where the camera latches onto individual fans, to convey the diversity of the crowd, the passion of fans, the reactions we are no longer capable of . . . Having done this, though, the person selected is also shown on a screen in the arena, becomes aware of being seen/shown, and participates, through waving, etc., and the camera pulls away. Does this illustrate an attempt by 'the system' to control the image? Or is 'the system' resisting full immersion in the morass of interactivity, 'spontaneous' reaction and mass-ification?

In any case, reality TV might be praised for democratizing access to the media, and answering some sort of wish for it to exist, but for Baudrillard, this high exposure for ordinariness highlights the bankruptcy of democracy, or rather, its future (p. 27), where its principle is too meaningless to be judged according to criteria of legitimacy. On the other hand, the raising up of the ordinary to stardom diminishes the faith in the usual star system, which relies on the faith that a star has done something or 'is' something worthy of fame and celebrity (p. 28). So Baudrillard passes through a recognizable critical perspective, only to end up finding a way in which the seemingly vacuous object becomes critique, but a critique which circles rather than probes its target.

Art and culture

The people, in the form of the masses, can provide a resistance to culture, a word that Baudrillard steers clear of, for the most part, as it is just as hyperreal as the social, only coming to prominence when it has lost all meaning and referentiality (i.e. reality). The Pompidou Centre or Beaubourg crystallizes his views on today's culture: at one level, the piece is an analysis of a new building, and a critique of a government trying to gain symbolic capital by chasing after modern art as it disappears or becomes something else. At another, he looks at how the building unwittingly demonstrates the new vacuity and populism of its society. The building should be empty, he writes (*Simulacra and Simulation*, p. 63; 96), as modern art has lost all meaning, and whatever residue might be left is bled out by the building itself supplanting, or *preceding* the art (a process taken even further in Frank Gehry's Bilbao Guggenheim, or Daniel Libeskind's Jewish Museum in Berlin). Beyond this, Beaubourg will be able to contribute to its and art's downfall, through its policy of open access (with its huge, free public library, its many separate service points, its encouragement of the masses to come, and above all, the absence of any interior walls), which will ultimately collapse it, as it cannot withstand being successful . . . The resistance, then, is not a refusal, but hyperparticipation.

Baudrillard wrote that in 1977, and in the late 1990s the building had to be remodelled, with walls put in (the people working there found the open spaces disturbing), the library and gallery functions separated (adding to queues, but controlling circulation), free access to the external elevators closed off, and the building's structural support strengthened. Baudrillard's injunction to 'make Beaubourg buckle' had been followed, even if, as he should have known, the masses weren't in too much of a hurry. Baudrillard is not being explicitly anti-populist here: the masses who would undermine Beaubourg's pedagogy include the mass-ified art lovers, experts and curators, all at least as stupid as those included in the more obvious connotation of 'masses' (uneducated, lower-class, lower-paid interlopers in art spaces).

Baudrillard is always contemptuous of the art scene, and increasingly seems to argue against the value or even the desirability of the existence of contemporary art. Among artists he does like are Marcel Duchamp, Andy Warhol and Francis Bacon. Duchamp and Warhol prefigure Baudrillard in commenting on the world without setting up a position of critical superiority. So, Duchamp brings manufactured objects into the world of art, disrupting the line between them, and undermining the way each operates. Warhol shows us nothing is original, in using found images, and repeating them, so there isn't even one single copy to stand as the work. Baudrillard does not provide a detailed reading of any artists, however, is strangely literal in his reading of them and his criteria for liking them are essentially to do with the assessment they provide of a world becoming the contemporary one.[2]

Baudrillard regards contemporary art's fascination with banality as being as empty as it claims to be, and therefore offering literally nothing, rather than a form which illustrates, criticizes or even tells us something about nothingness. Modern art essentially disappears as simulation replaces representation (he ignores abstract art, presumably as the last forms of what he might deem a worthwhile art involve attacks on representation rather than stepping outside it), and experimentation now goes nowhere.[3] Where modernist art still had an element of illusion, even in dismantling the way we saw reality, contemporary art is only interested in banality (*Screened Out*, p. 181; 205). It is transaesthetic, coming after aesthetics, and merging with other forms. The search for banality fails, he argues, because what we are shown is 'too superficial to be really useless' (p. 182; 206). It is in fact so dull and vacuous that we are forced to try to attribute some interest to it (p. 184; 208). To say 'that's the point' is to miss Baudrillard's scathing critique of banality as desired result. Such a project claims an ironic distance while pretending it does not want it: all of which makes it fail as banality, and become merely nothing. Warhol was truly vacuous, and therefore interesting (*Screened Out*, p. 184; 208), while Jeff Koons is a weak, non-parodic copy of Warhol, and his attempted parody of kitsch fails (*Cool Memories IV*, p. 92; 118).

Baudrillard targets new media, installations, performance art, naïve painting or drawing and art photography, but doesn't really go into specifics, or address how a particular art form is always and inherently feeble. For Baudrillard, like Adorno, modernist art was going somewhere, and everything after that or different to it is caught within recuperation by the art market, the mass market or both.[4] Nevertheless, although Baudrillard might strike a chord with those who rant against new art, he is not at all in the same camp. For him, all art is over (*Transparency*, p. 11; 19), so we should do something else, and the problem is that artists are only pushing art further into being its own simulation (and not in a 'good way'). His problem is that he does not look in enough detail at what artists are up to, and thinks no-one else has had this idea, much less that artists might have moved on from there. The art world itself has adjusted, and though keen to label things art in order to value them, is always expanding what can be called art (or what raises the question 'what is art'), in the same way capitalism must expand and find new products and markets. In the early twentieth century, new experimental art spent a certain time not being art before being allowed in. Today, someone like Tracey Emin does not have that freedom.

Difference

The notion of 'difference', understood in a myriad ways, has considerable currency in contemporary theory, and also in the 'real world', with the emphasis on respecting difference, whether it be in terms of race, sex, gender, physical attributes, even age. Baudrillard is scathing about this, insisting that the call for 'difference' signals indifference (*Illusion*, p. 108; 152). Appealing to difference as a positive marker diminishes whatever was different, as the otherness is subsumed, homogenized into the semi-racist conception of the melting pot. The contemporary world is a globalized one, where sameness is encouraged, and 'difference' merely fills the gap where the Other used to be. According to Baudrillard, it is our (the modern West's) refusal of alterity that spawns our nostalgia for the Other, who is now always already domesticated, mediatized. This can be taken back as far as the idea of the 'noble savage' reconstructed by eighteenth-century European writers. The 'savages' themselves had been wiped out, incorporated, or killed by disease by that stage, so could now be mythologized: the less aborigines there are left, the more there is nostalgia for their way of life, he writes (*Cool Memories*, p. 165; 145). It is Baudrillard's contention that we are living in a mass version of just such a nostalgic praise of difference.

Difference, especially in terms of 'cultural difference', is gener-ally seen as a positive rethinking of how the world fits together, free of hierarchies or presumptions that we should all adopt one way of living or thinking. But difference still differs from, and implies a number of fixed identities coming together and mixing, whereas culture is inherently this, and always ' has been.[5] Whites, Baudrillard writes, are the most mixed of all, and it is bizarre that they should praise others' difference, as it is based on a spurious presumption of purity (*Transparency*, p. 136; 140). He believes a heightened sensibility around 'difference' actually limits our thought and actions, with regard to 'others'. As a positive (and slightly contradictory) counter-example, he offers Brazil, where the races are so mixed that they no longer have separate identities (p. 144; 149).

Despite this possibility, we must reject the fostering of difference. He goes against the notion that any oppressed or marginalized group needs first to have an identity, and that identification will be exacerbated if 'difference is respected', as the marginal gets valued as such, therefore leaving the marginalized where they are. Baudrillard wants us to have a greater degree of otherness, and reject difference entirely: 'otherness [*l'altérité*] is not the same thing as difference. One might even say that difference is what destroys otherness' (p. 127; 131).[6] The other has symbolic worth, and engages us in a relation of symbolic exchange, but for this to happen, the other must stay Other, separate, perhaps difficult to understand, uncontrollable (ibid.). Perhaps the most striking example in political terms is how the West sees radical Islam – even the established theocracies like Saudi Arabia and Iran, or the application of sharia law. Strict application of Islamic law troubles the West, but a respect for difference mutes criticism. Islam today maintains its position as Other not just because it is different, but because it sets up a paradox for a world which thinks itself different to it, and slightly superior because of what it terms tolerance.

Baudrillard advocates a renewal of 'exoticism' where the other is of interest as other, as beyond assimilation (here he explicitly follows writers such as Victor Segalen, but also parallels the strange anthropology of Bataille, Roger Caillois, and more recently, Pierre Clastres and Alphonso Lingis).[7] Strangeness is what interests him as a traveller, and, clearly, attempts to understand the natives would bring accusations of simulated authenticity. The same problem occurs with someone being a 'traveller' rather than a mere tourist, with the difference being that the first doesn't know he or she is a tourist.[8] Once again, Brazil is praised, as somewhere that is radically different in its heterogeneity rather than in its identity (*Figures de l'altérité*, p. 105), while Japan also maintains an inherent otherness (pp. 95, 135).

His final position is easy to criticize, as his texts are full of what remain Western presumptions (and the same could be said of his European presumptions about America, notably in the eponymous book), although we could save him by saying that he is aware there is no way out of them, and that that is why we should try to keep the other as other. The criticism, though, receives further support when we look at what he has to say about sexual difference. Woman has been rendered different, domesticated through sexual liberation (*The Perfect Crime*, pp. 115–23; 161–72).[9] Difference means that Woman has lost her privileged relation to seduction, that which is outside the order of production (of meaning, truth, the real) (p. 119; 166). Baudrillard, unfortunately, does seem to be saying that it would have been better for feminism to never have been. As with his ideas on how we view cultural difference, the critique works up to a point, insofar as the insistence on difference is a limiting, not a liberating factor, as 'respecting women's difference' can end up recasting very old prejudices about sexed behaviours. We could also imagine a Baudrillardian critique of the use of 'gender' instead of sex – unless you have an option not to state your biological sex, it is only a simulation of what 'gender' is supposed to mean. Sex itself is always caught within a model of sexuality (this is what he means in his use of 'transsexual' (see *Transparency*, pp. 20–5; 28–32)). In this, he would not be far from Monique Wittig, Judith Butler, or Foucault. Overall, though, his take on Woman, or women, can be alarming, as, for example, he wonders whether the emphasis on sexual harassment demonstrates some sort of phobia about sex (*The Perfect Crime*, pp. 121–2; 168–70). Even when thinking of cultural difference, which will often imply race, or appearance in some form, Baudrillard can verge on the painfully traditional; in musing, for example, that blacks are sublime and animal, where whites are neutral (*America*, p. 16; 36). In short, the moment of critique of difference is a valuable one, but the detail is often worth avoiding.

Body

The contemporary world is one where the body disappears, according to Baudrillard (*Transparency*, p. 116; 122). Like reality, though, its status seems to have been enhanced, perhaps becoming a hyperbody. Essentially, his argument is that the body has been surpassed by DNA, cloning, knowledge of its microworlds, and viruses, one of which is AIDS. Individuals lose their physical uniqueness and autonomy as they join the endless stream of DNA, and they even lose their humanity, as the line between human and animal is effaced due to the high proportion of shared DNA (*Illusion*, pp. 96–7; 138–9). So now we perceive our bodies (and for some, our social behaviour) as products of chemistry, and a combination of fatalism and chance. DNA is initially our prosthesis, something to be added to our knowledge of biology (*Simulacra and Simulation*, p. 98; 148), but as we discover/invent more, we become the prosthesis, the residual product (*Impossible Exchange*, p. 41; 58) in a form of biological resolution of Bataille's conception of life as unnecessary, wasteful exuberance.[10] DNA is the biological realization of 'the code' that writes simulated society, and it is no accident it was discovered when it was: just as the unconscious belongs to Modernity, so DNA is part of something like postmodernity, i.e. it is a historically specific method of interpretation (*D'un fragment*, p. 49).

Bodies in 'primitive' societies circulated in symbolic exchange, whether through sacrifice, rituals around the dead, the relation of dead to living or the exchange of women (the latter only to some extent, as it is more accurately thought of as the basis for standard economic exchange, social hierarchy and economies of representation). In that world, bodies are marked, shaped, coloured, pierced, as part of symbolic exchange (*Symbolic Exchange*, p. 107; 164). This gets lost in the West, in particular, caught in the economy of representation, where signs are what count. Dress and marking become part of an exchange of signs, of social meanings (p. 95; 143), and eventually become immersed in fashion, where the signs are not even seen to carry inherent meaning (as they drive or create social subgroupings, rather than illustrate them). Fashion resembles an excessive economy, but it is a proliferation rather than an endless sacrifice (pp. 94–5; 143). It cannot aspire to the heights of the ceremonial, to ritual processes beyond the weak liberation of individual desires (*Fatal Strategies*, p. 178; 197–8). In the 1970s and 1980s, some sought to restore the sacred in relation to their bodies, get out of the system, and 'modify' their bodies through piercing, scars and body rituals based on violence and transgression of acceptable behaviours.[11] This occurred at a 'subcultural' level, linked to punk and to 'industrial' music, but was also going on in the performance art of Vienna in the late 1960s, America of the 1970s, and artists such as Stelarc, Mike Kelley, Gina Pane, Carolee Schneemann. Both performance and piercing thrive in the early 2000s, and tattoos and piercing have been incorporated into the mainstream to the extent that any residual 'outside' value they had in the 1980s has been removed.[12]

Perhaps we can see (contemporary) tattoos and piercing as prostheses: instead of an older symbolic (non-) value, they stand in for the lost reality of the body. Stelarc, who has experimented with very literal types of prostheses (suspending the body, altering its configuration; a third arm; bodysuits controlled by others on computers) is grafting an ear onto his leg. Here the body is given over to DNA (the irony here being that it already is, and Stelarc's intervention annuls itself) and DNA is made transparent. Developments in technology are altering our relation to 'the' body, but we don't need to go to the excitable world of retro body art to see this. The driver of the Formula One car is just as good an example: the car is initially his prosthesis, transforming him into a fast moving, wheeled cyborg.[13] But soon, the human is superfluous, and has to simulate the 'great racers' of the past – the driver is the prosthesis, the slightly cumbersome way of maintaining an authenticity to the 'sport' (*Screened Out*, pp. 166–70; 187–91).

From DNA comes another stage in the obsolescence of the individuated body: cloning. Our very first prosthesis was the double, writes Baudrillard (*Simulacra and Simulation*, p. 95; 143), and that has gone, as we seek to control the other through medicine, domestication, and rendering it the same, rather than excluding it as threatening other. Even our own bodies are not permitted to be other: mind–body dualism is no longer accepted by either advanced theorists or ultra-conservative cognitive scientists. We now identify through and with our body (*The Perfect Crime*, p. 124; 173), and Madonna is the archetype of this new relation: the body is not other but mouldable, as we are now free to express our selves bodily and mentally at one and the same time (p. 125; 174). Now that the body is safe from being other, why not make it even more the same by multiplying it?[14] Cloning literalizes the rendering same of the other. Death itself is controlled by our reproducibility, as opposed to being encouraged through reproduction and death (*Screened Out*, pp. 196–7; 223–4).[15] With cloning, the child is now a product, a prosthesis (p. 103; 116), fully modelled in advance, a hyperchild (and perhaps like Dolly, an already aged child). Critics of cloning imagine there will be some sort of drive to ideological views of perfection, or social hierarchy and exclusion based on genes (as in *Gattaca*), but what will happen, thinks Baudrillard, is a levelling out, more of a lowest common denominator humanity. Those in favour of cloning, and proponents of social construction, might argue that a person is not defined by genetic biology alone, and that culture will differentiate clones from each other. This is an error, Baudrillard believes, as it misses the role culture has as a cloning agent, as a means of homogenizing (*Impossible Exchange*, p. 37; 52).

Eventually though, our bodies, cloned or not, might be incorporated into machines for convenience: for health, we can all live in 'bubbles' that can protect us from the environment (*Transparency*, p. 61; 67); we can remodel our bodies, treating them as simulacra, all the while insisting on the realness of what we are doing (p. 23; 30), or we can adapt to new machinery by atrophying our physical bodies entirely. Baudrillard argues that the virtual human (although still an embodied one) will be physically and mentally handicapped (*Impossible Exchange*, p. 115; 146). This is not a conspiracy to control us; rather, it is the passive resistance to being exhorted to participate. When *The Matrix* has the entire human race preserved dreaming, and used as batteries, it ignores the fact that we might actually choose such a mode of existence.

Nature

Nature, like the body, is disappearing. This is because culture, followed by virtual reality, is taking over the world, emanating from California, as a paradigm of simulated culture (*America*, p. 126; 246), although culture reproduces fractally and continually, spreading from all points to all points. Nature has been seen as other to culture for centuries in the West, and therefore as something to be fought. But now nature is expected to be already tame. Contemporary culture might be harming the environment, but it is the fascination with preserving the environment that is most detrimental to nature. The ecological movement has been highly influential, but as far as Baudrillard is concerned, it misunderstands nature and our relation to it. Nature is supposed to be good in all its workings, and even killing is beneficial if deemed natural. But nature contains Evil, argues Baudrillard, or at least it should (*Illusion*, p. 81; 119). We try to minimize the dangers and struggles of nature, as we have become obsessed with survival rather than quality of existence and 'the fatal' (pp. 87–8; 127). The nature we should be preserving (through non-intervention) contains death and catastrophes. It also certainly contains extinction, yet here we resist evolution as its 'reality' is something outside our control.

Baudrillard's paradigm for contemporary nature is Biosphere 2, a controlled, domed multi-environment demonstrating the diversity of habitats of Earth (the Eden Project has a similar object).[16] It is not a representation, but a simulation of nature, sealing Earth off (p. 74; 109), and just like Disneyland, it is there to cover up the simulatedness of that which it is not: the rest of the USA, the

World, Nature (p. 87; 126). In other terms, in having a second bio-sphere (a prosthetic one), the first becomes secondary to its own simulation. Biosphere 2 excludes predators and viruses, for the very obvious reason of protecting the life in there, but, more importantly, this allows it to stand for our clean future, free of any-thing we didn't vet and introduce ourselves.[17]

Catastrophes and viruses take their revenge: the involvement of the greenhouse effect in our changing climate might be one such attack on human domination, but maybe it's our will to control the environment that makes us insist it is our fault. We expect earth-quakes and eruptions to have progressed like us (becoming more 'civilized'), whereas they resist sanitization. We cannot eliminate waste and destruction, but nature is wasteful, even down to DNA (*Illusion*, p. 102; 144). Baudrillard is not idealizing nature: there really is no such thing for us, whether there is a real nature or not. There is nothing, for us, fully outside culture, only things imagined to be, but they could at least be imagined as other, rather than known as part of sameness.

Viruses, at both biological and computer levels, are the system falling in on itself (*Transparency*, p. 64; 71). Cows with BSE take revenge for being meat (*Screened Out*, p. 172; 194). Baudrillard has referred on many occasions to AIDS, and tends to liken it to an inoculation: possibly 'herald[ing] a vital resistance to the spread of flows, circuits and networks – at the cost, it is true, of a new pathol-ogy, but one, nevertheless, that would protect us from something worse' (*Transparency*, p. 66; 73). It is also an 'antidote' to sexual lib-eration. This is worryingly close to conservative reactions to the illness, and to simple homophobia: it suggests that the illness is in some way a consequence of certain behaviour (liberated), which is a much stronger claim than it being a consequence of certain acts (which could still be contentious). We also have to wonder who the 'we' that is saved is: is it 'we' the general heterosexual, non-drug-using, non-haemophiliac, Western population, for whom the others are sacrificed? Even as an accursed share, this does not work, as it is too utilitarian and moralistic. Alternatively, maybe 'we' is everyone, and then Baudrillard would be suggesting that AIDS is for all of 'us' (this is nearer to his intent, I think, despite the possibly suspect moments in his references to AIDS).

The fact that he also includes cancer as something that saves us from a greater evil (*Transparency*, p. 66; 73) makes his point more consistent, if barely less potentially offensive. AIDS has a particular resonance in that it is deadly, but only makes the body turn on itself, rather than directly killing, and shows the fractalization of the body, or even the viralization of the whole body, as all viruses become stronger and evolve. Cancer, at a general rather than individual level, results from Western lifestyles in particular, but often also from historically unprecedented human longevity, health and lack of war. It too is literally the body turning on itself. Beyond these two illnesses lies the more creeping threat of viruses hardened by overuse of antibiotics and a pathological will to cleanliness in the West. Allergies have dramatically increased, and the resort to treatment for minor ailments has let illnesses develop to the point where many drugs are ineffective against them, or where the treatment required is too dangerous to administer to old, young, or, ironically or not, the sick.

What then would AIDS or any other violence or virulence save us from? It saves us from absorption into a total network, and becoming fully fractalized, submitting to a 'total loss of identity through the proliferation and speed-up of networks' (*Transparency*, p. 67; 74). Clearly a computer virus can directly prevent this, as we keep a distance from a fuller immersion into the virtual, but how would the non-existence of AIDS have made us any more 'lost in networks'? He has to mean two things, possibly simultaneously: first, sexual liberation is something he would like curbed, as it is apparently part of something else, a way of removing our last fragments of identity, seduction, capacity for symbolic exchange (or he just doesn't like it); second, AIDS here is not the real illness, but is a figure for 'virus', signalling the inevitable failure of our obsession with health, cleanliness and the exclusion of death. In this latter reading, though, there is still the limit that Baudrillard would have to take AIDS as a physical critique of all Western society, rather than the parts it affects most.[18] To summarize, in the abstract, the idea of viruses being the return of the other, or nature, is fine, but the comments on AIDS are to an extent problematic.

To give Baudrillard his due, we have to recall that *all* phenomena are assessed in terms of their relation to the hyperreal world, and viruses drive the fractalization of reality, the individual, the body and institutions, while also being encouraged by that very fractalization. The virus is complicit with all technology and liberation (of capital, ideology, knowledge, access to information and images on the Internet) and not just sexual liberation (and any liberation is a freeing up, not freedom) and medical technology.

Photography

The contemporary world is saturated by images and arguably replaced or restructured by them. Any image or set of images that purports to convey reality is supplementing hyperreality, in Baudrillard's view. The exception is photography, which acts as a brake on the narrating of the virtual world. As well as writing on photography, he has also, since the mid-1990s, been taking and exhibiting photos, which, while not intended as a demonstration of theory and practice coming together, are consistent with what he sees as photography's potential.

Photography should not represent, but should capture alterity, leaving the object its mystery. He writes that 'good photography does not represent anything: rather, it captures this non-representability, the otherness of that which is foreign to itself (to desire, to consciousness), the radical exoticism of the object' (*Transparency*, p. 152; 157). Photography is generally understood to be showing a reality, or to at least be a form that encourages the belief that reality is being shown.[19] Whether we are looking at people or things, Baudrillard is always after otherness, not familiarity, or the means of establishing familiarity. Of photographing 'primitive' peoples, he writes that it is not their identity that will be captured, but their otherness. Photography is the attempt to impose a subject/object relation on the world, where the latter is known to the former (p. 155; 160), but 'primitive' people resist, and face up to the camera in a form of challenge (p. 151; 156), while the photographic image itself also resists. *Anyone* (i.e. not just 'primitives') who has had little experience of the camera can provide such a relation, but today we have infected the world with the 'image virus' (*Photographies*, p. 149; 97). This position could still be criticized on the two grounds of suggesting that at some stage, photography quite simply did show some kind of real, and one day stopped doing that, and on the other of exoticism, and possibly patronizing assumptions about 'primitives'. Despite these misgivings, what he has to say at a deeper level about photography and its status in the contemporary world offers a model useful in its own right and in terms of what it says about the simulated and/or virtual world Baudrillard has us living in.

For Baudrillard, photography's interest lies in its display of illusion and strangeness (*The Perfect Crime*, pp. 87–8; 128–9). This comes about through its bringing into vision the disappearance of the object, and also that it is, as a result, 'the trace left by the disappearance of everything else' (p. 85; 126). It is worth pausing on this thought, because, for the most part, Baudrillard offers what seems a very conservative take on photography: it lets what is there be, even if in his case, what you get as a result is mysterious rather than revealing. What we also have, though, is a deconstruction of representation and that which would be represented: all we have is a series of absences, of realities missed, and realities that have always only disappeared. The nostalgia of a photograph is not for the object shown, but for the reality it never had, which is further removed by its maintenance as an image. When Baudrillard shows some interest for Barthes's conception of the 'punctum' as the space of interaction between viewing subject and image-object, gathered around death and absence, it is not a specific something or someone, or even death, that is to be missed, but everything, the world.[20]

Photography is the purest image, Baudrillard consistently maintains (see *Transparency*, p. 154; 159), because it excludes meaning, always works as a fragment, and removes anteriority (*The Perfect Crime*, p. 58; 88). The problem is that viewers do attribute meanings and realness in the case of apparently documentary pictures, and do try to construct a narrative of which the image is part. However, Baudrillard is right here, I think, because the single image still resists such a process of attribution. His own pictures try to avoid both representation and aesthetic value (*D'un fragment*, p. 136), the latter being the next thing a viewer will 'give' to a picture if it doesn't seem to fit into a story. Photography should not aspire to having a function: documentary pictures are caught up with a model of realism that dwells on misery and shows what should not be there, a sort of moralized reality (*Photographies*, p. 148; 96). So this 'realism' becomes an aesthetic of misery (p. 151; 99), where all homeless people have been photographed, for example.[21] Aesthetics is unavoidable for 'realist' photography (and it follows a closely controlled set of pictorial conventions), and meaning is unavoidable for art photography. Photography should keep away from art (*Paroxysm*, p. 89; 162). However, despite Baudrillard's vehement dislike of contemporary art, and his suspicion of art photography, photographers such as Cindy Sherman do seem to be playing with simulation, and others, such as Andreas Gursky and Jeff Wall, show something other than just the content or the display of the formal side of photography. A serious consideration of more 'realist' photographers such as Nan Goldin would also have to concede there is something interesting going on precisely when realist photography is brought into the gallery.

Baudrillard estimates that the intention of the artist-photographer betrays the image itself, and the absent world-object let through in an ideal image-fragment. His own pictures show empty streets, rooms, magnified details of mundane scenes and objects. The images are of a quality beyond what would be thought necessary for images of unrelenting banality, and, contrary to what he suggests, imply a painterly quality, and on occasion, the blurring of lines between photography and painting seen in Gerhard Richter. His own view is that this presentation of the object allows the world to appear ironically, always separate from itself (remembering there is no world-in-itself either) (*Photographies*, p. 126; 79), and that its fragmentary nature is *of* the fractal world, rather than showing it. This ironic falling back into the world is crucial in his own photographs, and allows him to avoid being a neo-realist (i.e. in 'letting objects be'), as all that is added is nothing, and in being added, the process of subtraction of the world, object, viewer and photographer is begun.

Digital media

Baudrillard has always eyed the digital world with suspicion, and as far back as *Symbolic Exchange* he insists that the 'code' (of computers, or of DNA) drives us further into simulation. More recently, it seems that the digital takes us from simulation into virtuality, into an interaction that is both more and less than simulation. Baudrillard's pessimism and general lack of interest in new media technology sit oddly with his emphasis on contemporary and future phenomena. The uneasiness and/or avoidance can be seen in his focus on the effects of the Internet, for example, rather than on how it works: 'video, interactive screens, multimedia, the Internet, virtual reality – we are threatened on all sides by interactivity. What was separated in the past is now everywhere merged' (*Screened Out*, p. 176; 199). In being called on to participate, we are no longer given the chance to opt out or to maintain any distance. The screen removes distance when we 'interact' with or through it, and demands immersion. As a result, we become terminals in a creeping virtualization. Curiously, Baudrillard rediscovers some pockets of non-simulation that are threatened by 'interaction': first, above, the notion that we were still capable of distance; second, the symbolic aspect of language:

> Today language is confronted by the hegemonic fantasy of a global and perpetual communication – the New Order, the new cyberspace of language – where the ultrasimplification of digital languages prevails over the figural complexity of natural languages. With binary coding and decoding the symbolic dimension of language is lost. (*Vital Illusion*, p. 69)

Is Baudrillard suggesting we still had some form of symbolic in language, or communication in general? This would go against what he has written for many years. Perhaps we could see this nostalgia as a commentary on the feeling induced by the arrival of an increasingly digitalized world: at that point, we notice the always already lost symbolic which only exists as absence. Maybe 'texting' is the kind of simplification and 'cooling' of communication he has in mind, but that would be far from the only way of seeing it: it could be seen as being a new kind of language – either highly inventive, or purposely moronic, both of which would be some sort of critique of hi-tech interaction. It could also be seen as retro-communication, with our phones increasingly taking us back to the days of the telegraph and Morse code, and our computers becoming telephones.

The Internet forces us to be part of the world, and not just a space with some sort of historic, personal or symbolic meaning: each of us becomes globalized. If the computer is yet another prosthesis that turns us into the prosthesis of the machine (*Screened Out*, p. 179; 202), then the world is also our prosthesis, and vice versa. We now have access to more or less everything, and are supposed to gain from this. We are free to discover more, create and interact creatively. Baudrillard, however, does not see us being freed by this: 'the Internet merely simulates a free mental space, a space of freedom and discovery' (ibid.). He is scornful of the idea that we can play with identity in the virtual. Instead of being free, we are trapped within code, beholden to it, and, in the end, have added more identity constraints than we had in the first place (*Figures de l'altérité*, p. 39). He has no time for the idea that the Internet can provide us with communities to replace those lost in globalization, or in alienation. The Internet destroys community, substituting a virtual community that is as compromised and futile as 'the social' in the 'real world' (*D'un fragment*, p. 112). He does not, however, make the claim that computers isolate you or make you lose your sense of reality, as neither of these have any meaning in an already simulated world.

Baudrillard appears to reject any notion of agency, any sense that the Internet and complex programmes that are actually easy to use democratize the production of simulation. Feasibly, he could argue that that would be a very small gain and would change nothing. Digital media are incapable of working artistically, as they remove all distance, all 'scene' where art happens (*Screened Out*, p. 176; 199). These views are consistent with his overall perspective on the contemporary world, but disappointing in not analysing the phenomena on their own grounds, or in not even looking much at the thing being criticized (this would be one way of Baudrillard spurning the exhortation to participate). Is there nothing to say about paedophilia and the Net, or about policing (for example, of sexual or terroristic intentions, deduced from what can be found on a hard drive)?[22] Surely there is something to be said that would echo the analysis of the Beaubourg as a self-destroying machine, in terms of the rubbish on, and numbers of users of, the Internet. He does look at the effect that 'real-time' coverage on the Net or

TV has on events, in that the real event can no longer occur, as it has no time or space in which to separate itself off (*Vital Illusion*, p. 65). This is, however, simply the same argument already put forward about events, and precession of simulacra. To sum up, the Internet, digital media, computer programs and games all take us into the Virtual, and that is all Baudrillard is really interested in here. His suspicion of the Net should be more widely held, but the lack of detailed attention can suggest a straightforward conservatism, rather than a counter-intuitive, polemical resistance.

Notes

1. Situationism came too early to know that participation would make the 'society of the spectacle' more, not less, spectacular.
2. References to Warhol and Duchamp are everywhere in Baudrillard, but see *The Perfect Crime*, pp. 75–84; 111–23, on the former, and substantial references to Duchamp in the same book (pp. 28–9, 76–7; 49–50, 113–14).
3. He praises Pollock, but insists that abstraction, 'in believing it was "freeing" the object from the constraints of figuration, to deliver it up to the pure play of form, [it] shackled it to the idea of a hidden structure, of a more rigorous, more radical objectivity than that of resemblance' (*Paroxysm*, p. 108; 193).
4. Baudrillard does provide grounds on which we can analyse contemporary art, and Arthur and Marilouise Kroker, and what used to be the 'Baudrillard scene' demonstrate this. The net journal *ctheory* still expands in a post-Baudrillardian dimension.
5. See Claude Lévi-Strauss, *Race and History*, which argues that no culture can be thought of in isolation, and that all culture requires crossings, intermingling, shared creativity.
6. Baudrillard echoes Monique Wittig, who argues (in *The Straight Mind*) that women should reject difference as it always *granted*, rather than a given, and therefore limits women to being a specific difference within a heterosexualist world.
7. This echoing is despite his mistrust of 'anti-ethnology', particularly that of Clastres (see, for example, *Le Ludique et le policier*, p. 346).

8. On this, see Baudrillard and Marc Guillaume, *Figures de l'altérité*, pp. 79–107.
9. As with many of his texts, this also appears, with slight variations, elsewhere – in this case, *Figures de l'altérité*, pp. 167–75 and *Screened Out*, pp. 51–6; 63–8.
10. See Bataille, *The Accursed Share*, p. 33.
11. While Baudrillard does not like this kind of art, it is arguably consistent with his theoretical texts, a consistency reiterated in *Télémorphose*, where he writes, similarly to Baudelaire, that it is what removes the body from its purported naturality that brings it to the symbolic or to seduction (pp. 19–20).
12. For some years, performance and/or 'body art' has pushed on: Orlan's plastic surgery, Ron Athey's violent recombinations of staged sexual violence, Franko B's pushing his body through blood loss. But these performances are caught in the simulation of 'extremity', and circle around the decay of the avant-garde in art, rather than being it.
13. See also Paul Virilio on the symbiosis of kamikaze pilot and plane in World War II (*Speed and Politics*, p. 117), as well as Baudrillard's take on J.G. Ballard's *Crash*, a world where broken cars and injured bodies combine erotically (*Simulacra and Simulation*, pp. 111–19; 163–76).
14. One way 'the' body can do this is through obesity, spreading to become the world. The scene of the body is replaced by the obscene of obesity (*Fatal Strategies*, pp. 31–4; 35–8).
15. Cloning even removes us from whatever validity the Freudian unconscious had, as the Oedipal triangle goes away (*Transparency*, p. 115; 121).
16. Biosphere 2 is enclosed, but was originally established to see how humans would get on in that environment (eight people would go in), thus tying it in to reality TV projects. The Eden Project, in Britain, is more explicitly an educational/tourist resource. Both offer models of cultivating future nature, as nature, rather than as crops. Pleasingly, you can also visit them virtually.
17. In addition to this, zoos have become the real habitat for some animals (*Fragments*, p. 27; 37).
18. Baudrillard is clear on AIDS not being a punishment

(*Transparency*, p. 67; 74) and that those who see it like that categorize sex itself as an illness (*Screened Out*, pp. 118–19; 133).

19. This latter is Roland Barthes's view in his 'Rhetoric of the Image', *Image, Music, Text*, pp. 32–51.
20. Barthes deals with this in *Camera Lucida*, which Baudrillard accepts as a useful view on photography, but not as important as Walter Benjamin's work (Baudrillard, *D'un fragment*, p. 147).
21. Franko B, in *still life*, may have escaped this trap in his pictures of where homeless people stay and sleep, but with them absent from the pictures, elusive and other again, because they are missing.
22. William Bogard, in *The Simulation of Surveillance*, attempts to account for changes in the nature of power and its implementation in societies dominated by simulation.

Chapter 6

Interview with Jean Baudrillard

The interview was conducted in Jean Baudrillard's apartment, on 17 April, 2003. Words in italics and inside quotation marks were originally in English.

Paul Hegarty: You wrote something recently about the war in *Libération* (10 March 2003).

Jean Baudrillard: Well, a month ago now – before it broke out, before it really started. Just before it started. Derrida and I did a session on the war together, so I said to myself I might as well go back to all that. Other than that, I didn't really want to talk about the war, once I had talked about 9/11, the singular event. The war was a non-event, but everyone – TV, radio – was asking me to talk about it. I said, listen, you haven't read my article where I say it's a non-event, and there is nothing to say about a non-event. So since then, apart from the article, I haven't got involved.

PH: I know it's a non-event, but it's impossible not to mention.

JB: Obliquely, mediatically, *'why not'*. The problem is what's behind the request – they don't like what I have to say, but they come to me anyway, because they need someone to say something different, the opposite of everyone else. Even *Libération* will publish an article, and then print the opposite view on the page next to it. An article appears, like a bubble – it's nice to do, but I'm under no illusions about the reception. You need to be in the right frame of mind, there has to be something going on – that's the difference between an article and a book. Or you need to be angry – not that I'm angry, I'm *'cool'*, but if there is something unacceptable going on, you need to demystify it, whilst keeping in some theory, if possible.

PH: Are you really trying to demystify something, or is it more of an exercise in writing for you?

JB: I think it's firstly an exercise for me, and that's how to do it. You shouldn't think too much about what's going to happen to it, as you can't do anything about it. There's not much response in any case. I know there is a reaction, but I only know about it indirectly. There are some who understand, and then some who pretend to understand, who'll say that it's great and then tell you the opposite of what you said. That's how things are.

PH: I've noticed that, especially among artists.

JB: Artists have always seriously misunderstood what I'm saying. That all started in the 1980s, with the American artists of the time.

PH: Do they have the right to do that?

JB: Yes. You let it happen. If you put something out you are in the hands of others – that's perfectly normal. It's also normal that there is a certain type of aggression against someone who writes. So you send it out, and something has to come back. It could be agreement, but it could also be an attack, like you see in some conferences. A sort of challenge. It's not a malicious attack, it's a bit symbolic.

PH: Challenge is still important for you?

JB: Yes, I think it needs to be played like that, played out as challenge, with the challenge itself as symbolic exchange, and not necessarily in terms of ideas, content, significations. You can oppose anything with ideas, they can stand in for one another, but there is a relation which is not personal, in psychological terms, and this is a form of 'challenge'. This relation has to be there – play, challenge, reversion. I believe it's an essential relation, and it's exactly what is missing in the current climate. Nobody thinks of responding in the strong sense of the word, as a challenge. People might try to refute, disqualify or oppose their ideas to your ideas to other ideas . . . but there's nothing really at stake. I hold on to it, but all of a sudden you're by yourself. Then the challenge is you against yourself, and you still have to play . . .

PH: And then there's indifference . . .

JB: Definitely – or the kind of tolerance that says 'I don't agree, but . . .', 'I've nothing against . . .', 'That's what we need – someone with totally the opposite view'. No – I don't want to be there as an extra. They say, 'we need someone to speak against', and immediately you can tell . . .

PH: . . . it's about legitimation . . .

JB: Exactly.

PH   What exactly is being legitimated on those occasions?

JB: It's about intellectual liberalism and difference. But then, you're being integrated, integrated as difference. If I want to set myself up as an antagonist, I don't want to be there as a difference, but the system swallows you up as one of all the possible differences: 'he says this sort of thing, we know him, he always says the same thing, he's an impostor' – it's often something like that.

PH: You're being allowed to do something, but you don't want permission.

JB: It's not acceptable when someone 'gives' you something in that way. One thing I won't be doing again is television – those programmes where there's a whole group of people invited. What happens there is everything gets swamped. At a push I'd still do radio, one to one.

PH: Do you watch much television?

JB: Not much, occasionally. I watch the news, but as I don't have cable, I don't get any of the interesting film channels. But I don't really care, I don't have much time to watch it. I've watched it a lot recently, even if what we see is intolerably trivial, banal, and the commentaries unbelievably bad. That's exactly what was interesting: that kind of banalization, in a continual loop. There's nothing to say about this event [the second Gulf War], because everything was played out in advance. It was still interesting. Other than that, I don't really watch it, except for a film now and then.

PH: But you still manage to watch some of the rubbish?

JB: I don't have any illusions about TV. I know what I'm going to get if I switch it on . . . I do like watching streams of images – and it's nearly always rubbish, and maybe that's what's most interesting on TV – things like *Loft Story* [French reality TV show]. I think that's the real TV. It's not really *Arté* [European, state-funded 'cultural' channel], cultural TV. There's the odd interesting thing there, but that's the world of the text really. Meaning is something else, and TV is just a conduit like any other. TV itself is destined for a sort of infinite proliferation – as banality, as a vague sort of interactivity, as vaguely hot reality.

PH: So is *Arté* a mistake? Should it exist?

JB: It's not a mistake. It's an indulgence. It's culture looking over what's left of itself. I don't see why not – I'm part of that world, I'm in all of that, so I wouldn't say don't watch it, neither would I say that it is quality whilst everything else is shit. Just take the shit for what it is. If I want to find culture, I'll make it myself, I won't look for it on television. But there are interesting things on *Arté* – interesting in the way a book can be.

PH: Isn't *Arté* a bit 'old Europe'?

JB: Totally. It's an extravagance, a museum. The cultural milieu has to have signs of recognition for itself. It already finds it hard to survive. I don't know what it's like in Ireland.

PH: Well, we're very 'cultural'. Just like everywhere else, with a recently invented traditional culture . . .

JB: Reterritorialization. But something is happening, there is some receptivity? There is a heritage, but is there a singularity? An Irish singularity, with regard to this global exchange of culture? I suppose that everywhere is a bit standardized these days.

PH: There might be. There is a claim of specificity, even though American culture dominates totally. That combination could be a sort of singularity.

JB: You see that everywhere. I was in South Korea not long ago. It was the same thing: they're ultramodern, there's been a huge boom, a flash, and it's fully mediatized, but what they're after is 'Koreanness' [coréanité]. So that's what they're looking for – in resolution, reconciliation with this global culture they fully participate in, which they're born with. It used to be a backward, poor country, and now it's taking off. But, what they're missing is 'Koreanness'. They go and ask Westerners to tell them what 'Koreanness' is, because it's not clear to them, not immediately.

Saying what it is is our business, it's up to us to invent it, so they come and ask someone like me what their cultural salvation might be. It's very nice, and they do it with a lot of courtesy. They are caught in the same problem, the same chiasmus, between the two.

PH: I get the impression from what you have written that Japan and Brazil are places where something can still happen.

JB: Yes, of course. Japan goes without saying; it has always been a highly singular country. Brazil, as well, but in a different way, is highly resistant, very strong. I liked the US a lot, especially in the 1970s and 1980s, and still do, but back then I liked it for its singularity – its anticulture, there's something about it, a form rather than a space. It is both the site of the global – deterritorialization – and original in its way. I liked that a lot, as something very specific. Now that's largely been wiped out – America itself has become global. It is both the epicentre and the victim of this globalization. Well – it depends which America we're talking about, as there are so many. Let's just say that it is less original, less interesting. I go there less, and more often to South America.

PH: Are you still going over to Brazil?

JB: I'm going again this May. It's not exactly for amusement, but it is a bit of an escape. I always go there for something specific, but it really isn't like work.

PH: Europe is very keen on South America at the moment.

JB: Argentinean cinema is breaking through. It's being heavily promoted, but down there, the Brazilians and Argentineans, are all looking to Europe. They still find it interesting, even though you say, hang on, it's much more interesting here. It's not just France they're interested in, it's also England, but French thought is still a kind of global heritage. It's listed as part of global heritage. I can't say anything against that, seeing that I profit from it.

PH: Will that last?

JB: I don't know. The audience for it is getting smaller. On the one hand, over the last ten years you have the invasion by American culture, Northern American culture, even in terms of the language. The French language is diminishing. There is still an element of privilege given to French thought, but less and less. Even in the US, there is major reduction in the potential audience, especially in the universities. There was never a real exchange, just, at one point, the mass importing of French thought. I went over to New York after 9/11. There we were, two French, two American intellectuals (although Americans are more academics than intellectuals), and they were there to settle scores with the French intellectuals. We were there to talk about 9/11, and I did, but I could see that everything had been done to avoid talking about the event. What they were after was a settling of scores. It was totally pathetic.

PH: There seems to be a lot of that – and in French thought, we seem to be going back to pre-1968 thinking.

JB: That's true. It started in the 1980s, with so many dying. It's not really a regression, it's a sort of reintegration, as we head off again towards earlier phases. As if to wipe something out . . . So we've seen the 'renewal', the *'revival'* of the Subject, values, moral values, the reinvention of politics – everything that got more or less swept away in 1968. That's happening every-where, including the US. A new fundamentalism [intégrisme] is emerging.

PH: It's surprising because in the English-speaking world, the 1980s and 1990s were all about 'theory', mostly French, and so we're all waiting for new ideas, and instead we get 'what is justice'. It's not even critique.

JB: I don't know what they're trying to get back. In reality it's not even modernity – well, maybe it's a form of modernity – humanist, humanitarian, but no longer in its ascendant phase. It's in its 'recycling' phase. Before, at least there was a straight line, always progressing, but now it's all over the place, like a spiral. All of which means that the current climate is stagnant, and largely disappointing.

PH: Which contemporary writers do you read?

JB: I read things that come out, but in a very unorganized way – I don't have any set reading. I stopped reading Bourdieu, I admire Derrida but it's not my thing, and the same goes for the 'sub-Derrideans'. There are some interesting writers – I like what Agamben writes, and also Žižek, who's not at all known in France.

PH: Who is obligatory reading in the English-speaking world . . .

JB: Obviously, yes.

PH: He's a bit too psychoanalytical for me.

JB: It is a bit too Lacanian – but still very interesting, and the text 'Welcome to the Desert of the Real' is very good. It's something I'd like to translate, I see where he's coming from, his vision of things, a particular kind of perception. I share the *'feeling'* of what he writes, whilst not agreeing with him at all. You can question it all: he wants to keep a sort of dialectic, there's still Marxism in there somewhere. He works with Jameson and people like him, with American neo-Marxists. Not forgetting the form of Lacanian real he uses. All of that is mixed in together, and there are all sorts of strange complexities. I don't know whether you can separate it all out, but it's very interesting – being very much in phase and also totally out of phase. There are exceptions . . . Sloterdijk has come through. Vattimo, but he's been around a while. English-speaking writers aren't well known. Some writers have an 'economy of reading', but I haven't had it for a while now – it's very much a secondary activity for me.

PH: Have you ever had any discussions with Chomsky?

JB: No. I haven't really had much discussion recently. Someone I know of, but hadn't met, was George Steiner, who was very friendly, very likeable. He has a certain type of cultured nobility, and very individual, insightful. We are hardly on the same wavelength, but that's not important.

PH: What about Michel Houellebecq, and his *Atomised*?

JB: It's the same sort of thing – fascinating, but a nasty sort of object. I find it suspect, but it's not him as a person I'm doubtful about. There's something about it I don't like. I don't know how to analyse it, although what I don't like is the complacency of it. Other than that, it's fine.

PH: Most of the best literature seems to be coming from America.

JB: It's nearly always better, and the same goes for the films – most of what I see is American. I'm not interested in amazing production or aliens. But there are films I like, like *The Truman Show, Minority Report* – not great films, but interesting. *Existenz* is good, even *The Matrix*. They asked me to do something on the new one, actually. They got in touch when they started filming it. There had been something on the simulacrum in the first one. This time they wanted to set up a private showing for me, and for me to write something on it. That kind of thing profession-alizes you though – I'm supposed to be in the virtual so it's me you need to go and see. Always the same misunderstanding – starting with the artists: 'What we're doing must be really inter-esting to you. You said the same thing.' The last ones were those 'biosymbiotic' artists [SymbioticA]. They kept pestering me, saying 'but you must love what we're doing'. I said, 'Hang on, this is not acceptable'. They have to get some sort of support, no matter how.

PH: That moment in *The Matrix*, where we see the cover of *Simulacra and Simulation* – it's a bit obvious, isn't it? Did you know beforehand it was going to appear? What was your reaction?

JB: No, I didn't know. I don't really care. Also, there were two ver-sions – and in the other that moment has disappeared. I don't feel in any way connected, or responsible for what might come about, as a result of my work. It's always been in the same in the US – there's an audience, and a sort of veneration, but negative – ever since the 'high priest [gourou] of postmodernism' and all that. They're fascinated by it, without doubt, as they write so many things about what I write, but it's always like the book reviews, or reviews of translations, in the newspapers, and always negative. It's either 'he's mad', '*insane*', or 'he's a *trickster*', a '*maverick*'. That's never changed since *America*, which they gave 5–6 pages to in the *New York Review of Books*, a major piece, but it was just to say 'he didn't understand anything about the reality of America'. Well, I reply that reality is not my thing. The book was very successful, and even burned once on a campus, which is the Holy Grail.

PH: Are you still doing photography?

JB: I had sort of stopped the last few years, but I've started again, as there's a show in Italy – 50 new, large format photographs, in Sienna. So I've been busy with that, and also another exhibition in Germany – Kassel – in December next, and one in Vienna. So I have taken up photography again. It's different from how it was at the beginning – it doesn't have the same character or inspiration. As well as that, it's known now, and people ask for it. I can show whatever I like, and it was never that that interested me, and all of a sudden you wonder what you are doing. When I take photos, I make images, and that's all. I'm not a photographer, nor a professional. Once they get circulated, go on show, obviously they take on a different meaning, and that's more or less inevitable, it's the same thing for books, but with images, I would say it's more outrageous. For me, images are more singular, more exceptional, more instantaneous, but that's over once you install them in a space for a period of time. Basically, I never quite stop doing it because I still like it, so I carry on. I haven't written anything new on photography, but I'm still attached to it, as a sort of counterpoint to writing, and even as something which has nothing to do with writing.

PH: Can you really separate them like that though?

JB: I have written on the image – the media image, the virtual image, and so on. For me, photography is the total opposite of all that – it's truly a sort of singular event, outside the system of representation and signification. That's what it was for me, but clearly, photography is there in art, in realism and in journalism. That is precisely what I have no interest in. It's more the object, imposing itself, rather than me. From that point on, there is no doctrine, because the object is without doctrine. It's there or not there, so it's more a suborning of an appearance, of light. I am after something similar in writing, but it's always a singularity, it doesn't mix. They are two specific, singular areas, which could have the same ultimate destination, but there isn't one, or if there is, it's always in opposition to the integrated circuit, the total circulation, of images, or ideologies, or texts. So, the attitude is the same, and there is a pattern, but I really don't think you can put the two together, at least not mechanically, just like that. A lot of people have wanted to see it like that, and immediately compared the two, and 'recognized' the link. I reply that they don't know anything because it's not at all the same thing. Then in the end I was forced to write about it anyway. I decided there was some sort of link – anamorphosis – between text and image, but not the sort of interactivity that's being used so much today.

PH: No praxis, either, I imagine.

JB: Absolutely not.

PH: When you say the object imposes itself in photography, that could be said to be a pretty traditional view, even if to say it in theory is radical.

JB: Maybe, but I'm not entirely sure. I go to a lot of art events and festivals, and although I see plenty of original or amazing pieces, I don't see much that hasn't gone via a subject, a gaze. Everyone talks about 'my gaze, my work, my thing'. There are very few photos or images where the photographer is just the means of staging a form of reality (which some of the time is totally unreal), or letting it happen, giving you something aleatory, that doesn't cohere. I have done some series now, but other than that, there's no theme or problematic being followed. Festivals and exhibitions have themes, ideas, and that all gets fixed at the outset, but my view is totally different. If you go back as far as icons, and the Byzantines, then you get the major distinction between *cheiropoiesis* – made by the hand of man, and *acheiropoiesis* – where something emerges from a contingency, or from the world, as it is – there's no human intervention, no human subject or voice. I think that's a good distinction, and the latter is what you get with early photography, when the machine lets the world break through. Now, though, that's less and less the case. And if you look at pictures of the violence in Rwanda or Baghdad, that's something else again. Is it photography? I don't know. It all depends on the definitions, the point of view you hold. Are they images? They might be photographs, but in terms of images, it's less clear. Barthes had some amazing things to say on this.

PH: Which still hold true.

JB: Completely, and not just in terms of the image – the event, for example. How does an event, even 9/11, keep its singularity? Thought has to try to sweep away all that came to cover it up, bury it, hide it away – including the [Gulf] war, obviously. It needs to dig things out, create a void around them, so that they can actually appear. So, it's true for the image, but valid for everything, I think. It's the same problem.

PH: Is it possible to be aware of what's going on, even if we can't fully capture the singularity of it?

JB: Yes, at a certain point, not in terms of reflexive thought or analysis, but more like a reflex. Even in photography, there is still someone there, certain things catch my attention, and there is an eye, some understanding. It's not a gaze in the accepted use of the term, but there is still clearly some sort of eye, and some sort of determining process. What you are exactly isn't clear – are you a vector, an operator? You are a kind of medium, but instead of the subject's will, you disappear as a subject, or as medium. There must always be disappearance of the subject and appearance [apparition] of the object. That's easy to say, and sometimes the subject only partly disappears, and in fact never fully does. There's an art of disappearance, and then, it's the object that helps you, and, in a way, does the work – so there's a handover of power, a sort of overturning. That is not so the object can become a new pole of gravity, nor is it a metaphysics of the object in itself. There's a game, and this game, at least, must be recovered, and the hold we have on things let go, but in the meantime, with technology – including the camera – the hold is getting ever firmer. Maybe there is a point where technology could go the other way. We can relinquish this hold, and at that moment, technology goes over to the object's side. That's what I'm after in photography – a kind of charm, in something that arrives from elsewhere, and free of any sort of personal story. All the literature coming out now is full of it – subjective, expressionist flights of fancy – we really are in Foucault's self-avowal. It's a culture of confession, where everything has to be brought out, avowed, confessed. All of that stuff . . . well, it's the dominant culture.

PH: Is this technological relation with the object the returning of the object's challenge, or is the subject in a position of loss in an exchange of objects?

JB: I don't really know. I see it as challenge, and I'm annoyed that so much philosophical thought – for example, the recent interest in Blanchot, and his death – is full of absence, discretion, the end of the subject – all of that is just platitudes now, and a given, and I don't think it can be – it should have to be played for. That thought was radical, was the best part of the nihilistic side of modernity. It comes in then, and that point – the nothing, nothingness, the void – can always make its irruption, and *that* is the interesting moment, but after that, it's all over. Now what you get is books that are extraordinarily intelligent, of very high quality, but of no interest whatsoever, because it's done, we know it. It's gone totally away from how things are going. You have the nihilist continuum of philosophy, from Heidegger on, centred on the problem of 'nothing', but all the while, things carry on, heading quite visibly and directly toward nothing, nothingness. What is the connection between the two? That is still interesting – you have the ultimate [philosophical] nothing, and you have 'nihil', nothing at all – a residue rather than nothing, and the residual world is heading for disappearance, disappearing in the virtual. Are these two the same thing? It's not the same type of disappearance, but once you've got a monopoly on the noble form, like philosophy has today, then the work is presumed to be done. I did that kind of thing before, but other things hold my attention, and philosophy, the way it's written today, really doesn't interest me. Philosophy has professionalized the void and absence, whilst others have done the same for the full and the operational, so there is a sort of schizophrenia there. I don't want to dismiss all of that – it's a good way, but somewhere along the line you have to find the other way. There has to be some sort of shock to the system, a clash, because, as we know, philosophy is supposed to always question itself, question its own absence, but that kind of thinking has become a complete positivity, a philosophical inheritance.

PH: The problem is with the followers – it's always the same stuff, even if the object changes.

JB: Absolutely. Yes – there's a recipe, an application, which isn't exactly a doctrine, but which does imply a certain strategy, and I saw that in the session I did with Derrida [on the second Gulf War] – he wasn't even really doing deconstruction. We ended up talking politics, which I've had enough of, but he had already gone on to that terrain. He has an oblique way of addressing things, which is full of insight, but with 9/11, for example, it didn't really happen – it's not an object for deconstruction.

PH: Although you could imagine something on the void, ground zero, what it means to reconstruct.

JB: It could be done – for example, on the theme of zero – 'zero death', ground zero – that whole global doctrine. I don't have any view about the architecture of Libeskind's project. It's fine, what he does isn't bad, but as for replacing it, if it was up to me, there is nothing any more that is worth destroying, so it's not worth building anything. It's an occultation – what are you filling up? – an empty space – it's the exorcists' way, a way of exorcizing things, and once that's the case, it could be good or bad architecture. The towers were not architecturally beautiful, but the destruction was, nonetheless, a beautiful event – war is always the opposition of event and non-event, and not at all some sort of political continuity, as if history still carried on – no, there is an event, and the rest is just an additional non-event, something to overcome the irradiation, the virus of the major event, of 9/11. After that, I don't see how political negotiations can work, and the idea it's all about oil . . . no, the fundamental humiliation has not been erased, and will not be. So, we are in an endless non-event. The event has a limit, it happens and that's it, it's over.

PH: Is it impossible to respond?

JB: Yes, impossible and unexchangeable. It's the impossible exchange – you can't get away from it. The curse of omnipotence is that it cannot be exchanged. Omnipotence is unexchangeable, because there is no more equivalent, and with no possibility of exchange, it starts secreting . . . in a way, it starts to destroy itself. That which you cannot exchange is unacceptable. You need to provoke an opposing, destructive force – which happens to be terrorism, and failing that, you have to fill the void with non-events, through force if necessary, but that can never erase the initial event. I believe this is a problem at a more general level – the unexchangeable, impossible exchange. We're all faced with this problem, in the most general way: what can or cannot be exchanged. We're faced with a world that is given, in the first place that's the natural world we find ourselves in. Previously, we could respond with sacrifice. In exchange, we had sacrifice. Today we don't have this possibility, instead we have this 'zero death'. We can't respond with that, and the Americans can't offer death for death, because for them what counts is 'zero death'. Whichever way you look, they're stuck. From there, either you have to destroy the world, as the world that is purely a given one, and to which you cannot respond, is unacceptable, or you invent a purely artificial one, and that's what I think the virtual is. Invent one that's not given, and that we have completely made ourselves. That would be *cheiropoeisis*. Then you do not have to account for anything to anyone, or to God. But that's not the end of it, because the world we create for ourselves still has the symbolic principle [règle symbolique]. The rule of exchange: once something is made, it must be exchangeable, that is, ultimately, it must be sacrificeable, a form of possible counter-gift. But with the virtual, the counter-gift is no longer possible. The virtual homogenizes, makes everything positive, so we find ourselves faced with the same, basically disastrous, catastrophic situation, which is 'what can we do with that?' How can we absolve ourselves of this virtual world we've created? It's still the same problem – there's no-one there to absolve us, and there is no more enemy facing us to justify our power [puissance]. The major task today is to invent one enemy after another – as in the 'Axis of Evil' – but it isn't working, it's more like the parallax of Evil – in other words, the 'Axis of Evil' comes back to the inside of the Good, comes through the Good, and they haven't understood that at all. We can't even ask them to understand. We're involved in a constant clamour that isn't even war – it's some sort of conjuration. We're getting to a point of total security, total prevention, like *Minority Report*, where all possible crimes are prevented. Anything that could happen, anything that might take place is regarded as terrorism. The rule, or the order, is that nothing take place, nothing is to occur any more. So anything that can occur must be predicted in advance, exterminated in advance. Suddenly, we have to redefine terrorism, because it's no longer just Muslims or fundamentalists – it's everywhere – it could be a natural catastrophe, or a virus like SARS – what we're talking about is objective terrorism. It's no longer at all religious or ideological . . . it's all forms. So, in practice, it's total war, maybe the fourth world war, or, like Virilio said, a sort of planetary civil war, as it's a coalition of all the powers on the side of order against all those who are now potential terrorists. All populations are virtually terrorist insofar as they have not yet been exterminated. That's what we saw in the Moscow theatre. So what can we do – the objection to all that is to say we need to reconstruct. Because of the shock to the system, everyone's trying to find the universal, some universal values which can mop up everything and mediatize it. Our Chirac is trying, against all the others . . . he brings up universal values and international institutions, but that's precisely the proof that you can't count on them any more. What we have is two extremes, extremists in opposition, and the universal got swept away by the world power which isn't at all concerned about it – we're in the global, not the universal, as I've said before.

PH: The universal still works in France . . .

JB: For us . . . it's our heritage. The only thing is, it doesn't have any value any more – it is not rated at the global level. It's not worth anything on the Stock Exchange, values are down.

PH: Even in the eurozone?

JB: There's always little islands of value, where it still goes on. That's the last resort, but at that point, it is no longer a transcendental universal, but a particular one that a culture cultivates for itself. We're using the universal as a strategy of returns [rechange], but it no longer has currency as universality – as a value it has disappeared. That's the situation as I see it, and for the moment, there's no solution, either. You can look for an answer if you adopt an intermediate level – a so-called political solution, but once you look at the symbolic level, there is no solution, because by definition there is no solution at symbolic level. There's a rule, a game, and you are caught within duality, alterity, without any possible reconciliation. What is interesting in the current situation is that we have got, violently, to duality. In other words, we are no longer in a dialectic, with its third term, but we are in a dual confrontation, and, that, I would say, is ultimately something good. It's progress, it's a radicalization. So we're a lot further from the solution, but a lot nearer the problem.

PH: And if you're too close?

JB: It burns.

PH: One last question: I'm very interested in the role of Bataille in your work – would you say he's important for your books since *The Perfect Crime*?

JB: Bataille, yes, Nietzsche above all – but they're not really reference points as such. I read Nietzsche in German when I was young – all of it, and since then I haven't opened a book of his. The same goes for Bataille – and in fact, it's better than a reference, as it's hidden away, part of the fabric, in the threads. I am Bataillean, even if I've written a critique of him . . . sovereignty, excess, the accursed share – these are still beyond domestication, unsurpassable.

PH: It's no longer possible to be Bataille, but if he were writing, he would be close to ideas like symbolic exchange, impossible exchange.

JB: Yes. Maybe there's some sort of mimetism, an analogism that plays unconsciously. That's at play, but I had the same effect on Barthes, some time ago. There was a sort of parallelism of subjects, themes . . . never looked for, but a certain type of complicity. I don't like the insistence on references – people are too fond of it. It answers the question too readily, and I've always tried to wipe out the traces . . . it's part of the work . . . so I don't really want someone to come and find them where maybe they don't exist, but with regard to Bataille, it's true.

PH: Is it better to live in a Bataillean world or a Baudrillardian one?

JB: I don't know. In Bataille's world, at that time, there was a form of excess, still something erotic, historical, in reserve – that we don't have now. I don't know what we live on. Unfortunately, it's precisely that world, made in the 1920s and 1930s, that we live on in. So in a way we are their successors. I still consider that something has changed, so the situation is nonetheless original. Original in its banality as well. There's a constant play between banality and fatality, but the circumstances are different now. There was a breath of air, an inspiration then that we have difficulty finding today. There was also a complicity – there was a big group of them, and they talked to each other. The group had a sort of 'mini-sovereignty'. That period is truly over. There's a fracture which meant there was something there, something of a golden age within modernity, even as it began to fall. You always have to be there, at the moment of fragility, the crucial moments of rupture, and they had the historic opportunity of an extraordinary moment of rupture. And we had 9/11.

Chapter 7

Before and After Baudrillard

Baudrillard wears his influences lightly, being increasingly less likely over the years to refer explicitly to theoretical precedents. He has not really dealt systematically with a thinker's work since *Forget Foucault*. Prior to that, Marx had been regularly and directly addressed, and Bataille had featured as an acknowledged theoretical precursor, and an important presence in Baudrillard. The earlier works inhabit a familiar discourse of intellectual analysis, with footnotes, exegesis, and structured, developed argument. Since the late 1970s Baudrillard has replaced this approach with a more fleeting, instantaneous engagement, where writers such as Canetti or Nietzsche feature briefly, suggestively. The range of references is, if anything, wider, but there is little to follow up in terms of potential comparative analyses. Baudrillard's writing attempts to live up to the promise of its being a thoroughgoing critique of all accepted systematic thought, and to leave the conventions of academic writing behind. The reference points are still there, not least in the stylistic echo of Nietzsche.

To some extent, Baudrillard is hoping for a form of creative theoretical purity, where any anxiety about influences is transposed into nonchalance about source material. We should not imagine there is anything casual about such an approach – it is more challenging to readers and writer alike to encounter what are often free-floating 'challenges' or 'provocations'. A reader of a range of Baudrillard's texts will, however, see a fractal system emerge, where each part is a part of the whole, with the whole a rendering of the part. It is tempting to bring the whole œuvre back to a conceptual base of simulation, or symbolic exchange, but the test is to make that attempt, receive Baudrillard's challenge, and then fail to bring it into an assimilable whole. Instead, we should try to see a play of meaning and wilful disruption of meaning, just as we are drawn to make abstract art or improvised music cohere in more regular, even if complex, forms. The same can be said of the major influences on Baudrillard. My own view is that Bataille's texts are paramount in understanding Baudrillard, and possibly also those of Foucault. McLuhan, Marx and Nietzsche are all also important, and the case can be made for any of the above being the major influence on Baudrillard. More recently, Virilio is both close to Baudrillard's interests, and someone Baudrillard actively engages with.

If we look at the influence Baudrillard's ideas have had (and however poststructuralist we may wish to be here, 'text' would be stretching it, as his notions float free of texts. If text there is, it is in its absence, possible like all texts), we would have to conclude it has been largely implicit. Even in art, where he has been highly influential, artists have followed Baudrillard's example, and not dealt with him directly and in depth. Even *Art and Artefact*, which is focused on Baudrillard and the aesthetic, is short of examples. Nonetheless, Baudrillard's views on art permeate pop art, hyperrealism (not always consciously), much work in the so-called new media, and inform a section of 1980s American art ('Neo-Geo'). This kind of diffuse effect is perhaps a result of the hermetic nature of Baudrillard's texts – like Bataille, Baudrillard resists being put to use, at least properly, faithfully, accurately. Baudrillard has to be taken as an object which makes you make another one, unlike Foucault's toolbox. Few theory writers have gone on from Baudrillard, which may indicate that his work is some kind of endpoint or a false ending, beyond which we continue purposelessly. Or he's so wrong as to be literally useless. In a way Baudrillard might like that, but sadly for him, the empirically observed world is fighting back and matching Baudrillard's vision. Some commentators have gone beyond Baudrillard – Arthur Kroker and Gary Genosko among them – but this has generally been through splicing Baudrillard with others, or colliding his ideas with current events, paralleling Baudrillard himself. Finally, current events have influenced Baudrillard significantly more than his peers, and in fact one particular event arguably constitutes the major impetus for his theoretical trajectory.

1968

The student revolt of May 1968, accompanied by a general strike, arguably changed the direction of French thought, particularly with regard to Marxism. Although Foucault and Derrida had been heading away from it, many remained faithful to Marxism's utopianism.[1] May 1968 exposed official communism as a dogmatic organization which merely reflected the power of capitalism – trade unions and the French Communist Party took over, and started demanding pay increases, better conditions, thus undermining the initial revolutionary impetus of the movement. The failure of so-called revolutionary organizations to be revolutionary when it counted created mass disillusionment and political violence was the resort of many. Intellectuals took May 1968 as a signal not just to dismiss Marxism (so goes the contextually determinist version of the story), but to reject all 'dogmatic' systems of thought, such as psychoanalysis, or any thought that insisted on a set outcome as the ultimate aim. Baudrillard provided a series of extended critiques of Marxism in the wake of 1968, and also gradually rejected psychoanalysis. He also moved to deal with phenomena hitherto not addressed by 'critical' or political theory. In this, he is with the thwarted students (as shown in the early utopian dimension to symbolic exchange), or even the idealist, leftist terrorists of the 1970s, rather than those who rushed into the potential vacuum, and analyzed 1968 until everyone was happy again, the improper challenge buried. In some ways, Baudrillard still maintains the hope of 1968, in its capacity to disrupt, if nothing else (as in his assessment of major events, catastrophes, terrorism, alterity).

Georges Bataille

From *Consumer* on, Bataille's thought permeates Baudrillard's texts. Bataille's 'accursed share', based on waste, destruction, sacrifice, transgression and eroticism, is the base for Baudrillard's critique of a capitalist society based on the simulation of an absent reality, which becomes an even more totalized, limited world than ever before. Baudrillard updates Bataille's critique of capitalism, incorporating technology to a necessarily greater extent. On the other hand, Bataille's transgression is no longer possible – there is no way out (which, arguably, Bataille knew full well), no act that cannot be resold, incorporated, sanitized, mediatized. He represents the end of an explosive modernity, but whatever came after modernity is about implosion, density, flatness, banality. Any attempt to literalize transgression will just bring it fully into the realm of simulation. Possibly Baudrillard is too hasty in closing off the explosion, particularly as some of his relatively recently developed concepts like 'impossible exchange' and 'the perfect crime' are 'anticipated' in Bataille. Bataille can be seen at work in *Consumer* and *For a Critique*, as a support for Baudrillard's attempt to rethink economic critique after Marxism. *Symbolic Exchange*, although it only has a small section directly on Bataille, is a continuation of Bataille's *Accursed Share*. *Transparency*, with its exploration of the system's momentary collapses, shares the purpose of Bataille's writings. A key text in Baudrillard's reading of Bataille is 'When Bataille attacked the metaphysical principle of economy'.

Friedrich Nietzsche

Like Bataille, whose texts are full with Nietzsche, Baudrillard follows Nietzsche in both form and content. Nietzsche's assertive, aphoristic style permeates Baudrillard, particularly the *Cool Memories*. Like Nietzsche, he is polemical, philosophically nihilistic (as opposed to the world, and rational readings of it, which are unreflectively nihilistic), and has a sense of lateness, of arriving after whatever was actually happening. Nietzsche 'prefigures' notions of simulation, notably in *The Twilight of the Idols* and *The Will to Power*. Both raise the question of why everyone is so interested in the real: 'the true world is supposed to be the good world – why?', asks Nietzsche (*The Will to Power*, §578). Baudrillard will ask this question forcefully when challenged about his claim that the Gulf War did not happen. Some, such as the Nazis, mistook Nietzsche's assertions about the fundamental falsity of everything to imply a total freedom of actions, but 'nothing is true, everything is permitted' signals that the world is only possible because there is no such thing as ultimate or actual truth. Baudrillard's notion of 'the perfect crime' reiterates this, as he argues that in making the world more and more real, we are destroying it as world, as possible real. Simulation is the contemporary form of imagining there is a true reality. Nietzsche, like Baudrillard, insists there have only ever been different ways of making such a mistake: 'the antithesis of the apparent world and the true world is reduced to the antithesis "world" and "nothing"' (*The Will to Power*, §567), and 'we possess no categories by which we can distinguish a true from an apparent world (there might only be an apparent world but not *our* apparent world)' (§583).

Marshall McLuhan

Equally important, and more explicitly so, to the theory of simulation, is McLuhan, who, like Nietzsche, can be seen as being updated and/or echoed in Baudrillard in both form and content. As Genosko has pointed out, Baudrillard does not always approve of McLuhan (*McLuhan and Baudrillard*, p. 76), but the Baudrillardian world-view, and indeed the communications-dominated world we live in is there in McLuhan in the 1960s, whether writing of 'hot' and cool media, the 'medium is the message', the global village, the 'tactile', or in more general terms how our conceptualization of the world drives what it becomes. The major work of relevance is *Understanding Media*, with its claim that the development of new media is essentially what drives human history (media can be transport media, linguistic media, war media, or even all technology, at a push). The major difference is in outlook. Contrary to what early critics of Baudrillard claimed, he is not an 'apologist' for today's highly mediatized society. Neither is McLuhan, but for the latter, technology could offer the prospect of a better society. For Baudrillard, technology becomes more interesting as it eludes us and gets beyond our control. He is fundamentally not interested in the purposeful outcomes we may or may not wish to make technology serve.

The *Medium is the Massage* and *War and Peace in the Global Village*, both produced with Quentin Fiore, point to many issues raised by

Baudrillard (technology, war, TV, fashion, politics when politics is no longer possible). The style of these texts, with the attempt to move on beyond the linear book (the text of both is broken up by images, quotations at the side of the main body, displaced statements and a continual crossing of genres and references) signals what Baudrillard tries to do at a theoretical level.

Michel Foucault

Baudrillard's debt to Foucault is easily overlooked, but he sees his writings as being in some way an extension of Foucault. The 'orders of simulacra' represent a periodization very much in the style of *The Order of Things*, and Foucault's conception of the centrality of 'discourse' not as a description of the world but as the thing that effectively makes the world, can also be seen in how eras dominated by different simulacra have no reality outside that simulatedness. Baudrillard's *Forget Foucault* is full of praise for its subject, and the 'forgetting' is not a rejection, but an exhortation to 'creatively forget' him, as Nietzsche would say. In other words, subsume him, and move on. Baudrillard's contention is that Foucault is right about the omnipresence of power, but this very omnipresence means power's time is over. Baudrillard's attitude to desire and sexuality is very close to Foucault – both deny that sex is either the means or the end of freedom. Both hold out, nostalgically, perhaps despite themselves, for a lost real, or a lost eroticism, which both get destroyed in our realization and visualization of everything. This 'lostness' can also be seen in both writers when they deal with exclusion of the 'other' (or all otherness). In Foucault, the modern era is one based on excluding the mad, the criminal, the sexual – only to make entire societies mad, criminal, sexual, and trapped as if in a prison. Baudrillard, in *Symbolic Exchange*, extends this to something even more fundamental: death. The modern era rejects all that is to do with death and decay, but as a result is obsessed by it (in the form of health on the one hand, and ultraviolence on the other).

Paul Virilio

Virilio differs from other 'poststructuralists', or contemporary theorists in general, but does so in parallel to Baudrillard. Baudrillard and Virilio see the world increasingly devoid of subjects, agency or controllable objects. In Virilio's *Speed and Politics*, speed and movement take on their own reality, in excess of reasons for, or methods of, speed. Virilio is fascinated by technology, and also warfare (on which, despite a superficial similarity, they have disagreed, as Gane has noted). His is a more spatially-based philosophy, which comes from his work in 'urbanisme' – the French, theorized, version of urban planning, but Baudrillard's recurring interest in architecture suggests many parallels between the two. Of all contemporary writers, it is with Virilio that Baudrillard has most dialogue.

J.G. Ballard

Ballard's detached observation of a world destroying itself through its own excess, whether in the catastrophic books of the 1960s, or the 'normal' elements of society revolting through or because of their hypernormality in the late 1990s and 2000s, is very close to Baudrillard. *Simulacra and Simulation* has an essay on Ballard's *Crash*, but as well as that, the analyses of hypermarkets and satellite towns, the museum for the end of art (the Beaubourg/Pompidou Centre), in the same book, are totally Ballardian. In return, Ballard pre-empts Baudrillard's ideas about the Gulf War in his short story 'The Secret History of World War 3' (*War Fever*, pp. 23–32), where Ronald Reagan's medical condition fills the news, while World War 3 comes and goes, without ever really happening. Ballard (like many of the figures in his novels) has done all that we can do faced with simulation: observe it, and adopt a radical passivity, be radically immersed.

Elias Canetti

Canetti's notion of a stalled history that we do not know has stalled recurs in Baudrillard's writings of the 1990s and 2000s, and is the primary source for the concept of history in *Illusion*. Baudrillard, though, is not examining a fully-fledged theory, nor does he go into a detailed analysis of Canetti. The source text is the following short, aphoristic passage:

> A tormenting thought: as of a certain point, history was no longer *real*. Without noticing it, all mankind suddenly left reality; everything happening since then was supposedly not true; but we supposedly didn't notice. Our task would now be to find that point, and as long as we didn't have it, we would be forced to abide in our present destruction. (*The Human Province*, p. 69)

As Butler points out, Baudrillard has no interest in any 'task', as it is no longer possible to find what was lost (*The Defence of the Real*, p. 149). On the other hand, he is indebted far more to Canetti than the one reference, however often repeated. Although collections of musings or aphorisms share a strong family resemblance, *The Human Province*, covering the period from 1942 to 1972, could well be an early *Cool Memories*. Like Baudrillard, Canetti has a jaundiced view of his surroundings, writes highly speculatively, while also being ironically dogmatic (i.e. nearly every paragraph is assertive, but there are many contradictions). The similarity does not end at a formal level – Canetti's ideas permeate Baudrillard at a subtle level. The former looks for the mystery of appearances he thinks is being removed in the contemporary world, muses on the fate of God when not able to exist, and returns several times to the notion of a society without death. The tone is also remarkably similar: 'we are coming from too much. We are moving towards too little' (*The Human Province*, p. 61).

Canetti also wrote the quasi-anthropological *Crowds and Power*, which strongly recalls Bataille and his Collège de Sociologie, as well as the now much less-read J.G. Frazer. This is a highly assertive book, this time full with portent and certitude rather than irony. Its interest here is that it could be seen as a bridge between Bataille and Baudrillard, particularly in the first section 'The Crowd' (pp. 15–105), which concentrates on modern crowds. Canetti eschews even concepts like the masses, to build an image of an entity without agency, that is the gathering of a whole array of forces, altering according to circumstance. These crowds are fatal, coming from nowhere, but inexorably coming to exist. Mostly, though, it is a much more Bataillean model that dominates, as packs and groups of humans lose their separation from animals and nature (which also recalls Baudrillard's notion of symbolic exchange). What ultimately separates *Crowds and Power* from either Bataille or Baudrillard is that it is too rational at a formal level, too systematic, and too compromised by notions of the 'primitive' being simplistically truer or more revealing of human truths.

Arthur Kroker

Kroker, along with Marilouise Kroker, and, on occasion, David Cook, is one of very few writers who have left postmodernism behind, and developed an ultramodernist way of thinking that engages with new science, new fashion, and the minute details of the contemporary. He draws on Nietzsche, Bataille, Foucault and Marx (less so the last now) as well as Baudrillard who is the central figure for this 'postmodern scene' that surpasses postmodernism. Kroker continually seeks to link Baudrillard's thoughts to current aesthetic, political and technological developments – and recently, the major forum for this has been the web journal *ctheory*. Baudrillard himself is not too pleased by the emphasis on transgression and challenging simulation through excess, but Kroker's work is a natural, excessive extension of Baudrillard.

Contemporary art

Baudrillard's significance is often taken as a given in the art world, yet precise use of his work is rare. From general (or should that be generic?) works, we find the following sort of statement of Baudrillard's place: 'in the 70s, artists reacted critically to the onslaught of secondary images and illusions in which the Baudrillardian *simulacrum* came to replace primary tangible reality' (*Art of the Twentieth Century*, vol. II, p. 561). In the 1990s, we see 'much art directed against art, against the "fiction" of the autonomy of the arts and their authenticity, in the wake of the ubiquitous Baudrillard' (*Art of the Twentieth Century*, vol. I, p. 393). Robert Hughes, while acknowledging Baudrillard's shady presence, is much more sceptical, writing of 'an Artworld cult-figure' (*American Visions*, p. 604). For Hughes, Baudrillard has committed two crimes: first, being a French thinker, and second, inspiring the 'Neo-Geo' movement of the 1980s:

> the main text-source for Neo-Geo was a French *philosophe* Jean Baudrillard, whose endgame vapourings about the disappearance of reality into simulation made him a talisman for artists and critics in the 1980s who could not imagine transcending the banal discourse of mass media. (ibid.)

Baudrillard himself is scathing about contemporary art, often on the basis of very little direct engagement with it. Art's counter-gift, or challenge, to Baudrillard is to misrepresent his ideas. The 'Neo-Geo' movement sought to look at iconic elements of modernism, and in Peter Halley's case, initially at least, this was in the form of geometry, with his ultra-geometric pictures, coloured in frivolously bright colours. Others took objects, whether from low or high culture, and reproduced them, sometimes with a new dramatic veneer (Koons), sometimes close to the original (Sherrie Levine, Richard Prince). While it would be difficult to imagine Baudrillard taking any of that seriously, Halley, at least, has a firm grasp of Baudrillard. He is also willing to question the application of the notion of simulation ('Nature and Culture', p. 1074).[2] The problem is still there in the art itself, because it is unclear that simulation can be used. A Baudrillardian artist would more likely use simulation or the virtual to try to evade them (and not criticize them), or even avoid them entirely.

An important strand of 1980s art, as it has persisted and acquired market and cultural values, is 'appropriation art'. Beyond the moronic use of popular culture in Koons is the work of Levine. She has taken modernist images, remade them, (re)photographed them, reproduced them. The critics take this to be 'simulation art', as the originality of the original is questioned. Except it is not: the original is constantly referred to in its originality (even if this is supposedly lost) by the new work, and the new work is a copy, not a replacement. Richard Prince takes images that have a different public – advertising, cartoons, press photographs – and 'appropriates' them. This, too, apparently, is a critical artistic take on simulation. It could well be that, but it has little to do with Baudrillard, and in the long term, these challenges fall back into the real art world, bought and sold, exhibited, criticized 'as if' they were real.[3] Maybe art criticism is where Baudrillard's ideas can be partially applied, but for the most part, the critical use has been as casual, or as limited, as that made of the ideas by artists, and as restricted to a minimal awareness of 'simulation' (just as deconstruction is in common critical and artistic use).[4]

Notes

1. For anyone familiar with the anarchist critiques of Marx and Marxism, from Proudhon in the 1840s, Bakunin in the 1870s (who also predicted Russia and Spain would have revolutions, while Marx dreamt of Germany and Britain having them), through Kropotkin and Emma Goldman, to Murray Bookchin, it is astonishing how anyone took Marxism at its word, and even more so in the English-speaking world, where, academically, it took off in the 1970s).

2. For his comprehensive reading of Baudrillard on simulation, see 'The Crisis in Geometry', *largeglass.com*. 'Nature and Culture', in abridged form, is in Charles Harrison and Paul Wood (eds), *Art in Theory*, pp. 1071–4.

3. As Baudrillard is sometimes aware, photography raises the same kinds of questions as his theorizations of the contemporary world, but perhaps even closer are Jake and Dinos Chapman's etchings on Goya etchings.

4. See David Carrier, 'Baudrillard as Philosopher, or the End of Abstract Painting', in Gane (ed.), *Jean Baudrillard*, vol. IV, pp. 20–36. This essay barely mentions Baudrillard's writings on art, and certainly does not offer a Baudrillardian perspective on abstract art, even to criticize it. See also Carter Ratcliff, 'The Work of Roy Lichtenstein in the Age of Walter Benjamin's and Jean Baudrillard's Popularity', in Gane (ed.), *Jean Baudrillard*, vol. IV, pp. 49–66, which also fails to deliver on its title, even though the essay's starting point, on Lichtenstein's recasting of art history in his own style, could have done.

Chapter 8

Conclusion: Singularity

Baudrillard's thought is ever more hermetic as time passes. Within his thought the resistances that are hinted at are swallowed up in the totalizing of simulation, and, later on, in the virtual. Yet Baudrillard never seems to face the impasse that a reader oriented to use-value might have when facing his texts. The non-systematic thinker, despite having what seems like his own universe, is continually prey to the world in its singularity. Baudrillard's theory attempts to match that singularity, and every time it looks like that theory can be reduced or assimilated, it moves on. In this, 'singularity' follows all the other concepts in Baudrillard: they occur within the world, alter the world, and also regularly transform his own theory anew. To be singular, for the writer, is perhaps to be outside the virtual, but not to believe yourself free of it. It is to be irreducible, always against, and maybe also impermeable. To be singular is also about staying apart, becoming definable only in your own terms (and these are not properly yours as you are beholden to them):

> singularity becomes its own horizon, its own event. It no longer has any definition or equivalent. It is reducible only to itself, rather like those integers which are divisible only by themselves. Singularity is a "unique sign", as Klossowski says – and a sign without content. (*Impossible Exchange*, p. 130; 165)

Singularity is not about choice or subjectivity, though. Buildings can be described as singular, and this is applied to the World Trade Center and Biosphere 2 (*Singular Objects*, p. 4; 14). What could have appeared like a renewal of individuality is undone, as once past the superficial equivalence of 'singular' and 'unique', we notice that these two constructions are part of a duality: the World Trade Center had its twin towers, Biosphere 2 exists in some sort of dialectic with Biosphere 1 (Earth). Both create an absence: the twin towers annul the Manhattan skyline, Biosphere 2 removes the primacy of the first version, as now the Earth is not the sole biosphere, and therefore no more a biosphere than the new one. Singularities do not, according to Baudrillard, fit a body of rules or into a particular domain, nor can they be analyzed:

> You have an object that literally absorbs you, that is perfectly resolved in itself. That's my way of expressing singularity . . . And it's essential that at a given point in time this singularity become an event; in other words, the object should be something that can't simply be interpreted sociologically, politically, spatially, even aesthetically. (*Singular Objects*, p. 67; 103–4)

Jean Nouvel, with whom Baudrillard is talking, interprets this as suggesting that certain objects are singular, and better for it, but Baudrillard counters this, reiterating the importance of 'the event': 'at first, we don't know whether an object will become singular or not. This is what I referred to previously in terms of "becoming", of becoming – or not becoming – singular' (p. 68; 105). Architecture, or any other object, must become an event, surpass its status as object to be seen and become an object almost beyond understanding. Clearly, the destruction of the World Trade Center constitutes its continued becoming, as does its absence. The event, as something which disrupts the 'real' world, is singular, uncontainable in its eventness (*Paroxysm*, p. 51; 96) even if the machinery of the media try to swallow it in 'real-time' coverage (*Impossible Exchange*, p. 132; 167). When that occurs, the event becomes non-event.

Singularity does occur, though. Events make the world singular, even if the world has been doubled out of existence long ago. Singularity is a condensation of the energy of events, and even of simulation, such that it collapses on itself like the singularity of the black hole: 'stripped of self-being, singularity therefore exceeds all our modern vision, novelistic or theoretical, which is a vision based on alienation and on the appropriation and disappropriation of self' (*Impossible Exchange*, p. 131; 165–6). I have argued earlier that Baudrillard sees the contemporary world as one of density, one where the masses swallow all, where the real is one homogeneous mass itself. Here, singularity is a heightening of that density, such that there is resistance. A resistance of nothing against nothing, as 'if singularity is bound up with becoming, that is because it is nothing in itself' (p. 131; 166). Singularity is not of the real, but of what is destroyed in the perfect crime (of real-izing the world, and ultimately making it hyperreal, then virtual). At first, singularity seems to be outside simulation, a location of otherness (as seen in the interview above), or an object or theory that stays apart, repelling approaches through the force of its density. Singularity, though, is a nothing that lurks within simulation, within what is known as the real. When it is attained it is both by accident and by fate (*D'un fragment*, p. 129), so although theory can become singularity, it can only do so as it becomes event, as it leaves the control of the writer.

Finally, singularity is 'bound up with the Eternal Return' (*Impossible Exchange*, p. 131; 166). The eternal return is Nietzsche's most radical view of subjectivity. In it, we are condemned to repeat every single moment, infinitely. Every moment has already occurred and is yet to occur. Each moment is a singularity, utterly closed, yet infinitely becoming itself. The subject never actually comes to be, although we devise a linear conception of time to combat the horror of the eternal return (see *The Will to Power*, particularly §617). In terms of simulation, what if each particle of hyperreality is in fact a singularity? Then behind each moment of nothingness lies another nothingness – the perfect crime is no longer single, but singular, infinitely. The reason singularity eludes simulation, then, is because it can never be, never real-ize its becoming. This thought is, in turn, the singularity of Baudrillard, and is only possible in the cool light of those objects that present themselves in and after simulation. The singularity is not timeless, but of time, and comes from trying to understand the challenge of now, and then challenge it back.

Bibliography

Baudrillard: in English

America, London: Verso, 1988. Translation by Chris Turner of *Amérique*.

Baudrillard Live: Selected Interviews, London and New York: Routledge, 1993. Edited by Mike Gane.

The Consumer Society, London: Sage, 1998. Translation by Chris Turner of *La Société de consommation*.

Cool Memories, London: Verso, 1990. Translation by Chris Turner.

Cool Memories II, Cambridge: Polity, 1996. Translation by Chris Turner.

Cool Memories IV: 1995–2000, London: Verso, 2003. Translation by Chris Turner.

The Ecstasy of Communication, New York: Semiotext[e], 1988. Translation by Bernard and Caroline Schutze of *L'Autre par lui-même*.

Fatal Strategies, New York: Semiotext[e], 1990. Translation by Philip Beitchman and W.G.J. Niesluchowski of *Les Stratégies fatales*.

For a Critique of the Political Economy of the Sign, St. Louis, MO: Telos, 1981. Translation by Charles Levin of *Pour une critique de l'économie politique du signe*.

Forget Foucault, New York: Semiotext[e], 1987. Translation by Nicole Dufresne of *Oublier Foucault*.

Fragments: Cool Memories III: 1991–1995, London: Verso, 1997. Translation by Chris Turner of *Fragments*.

The Gulf War Did Not Take Place, Bloomington, IN: Indiana

University Press, 1995. Translation by Paul Patton of *La Guerre du Golfe n'a pas eu lieu*.

The Illusion of the End, Cambridge: Polity Press, 1994. Translation by Chris Turner of *L'Illusion de la fin*.

Impossible Exchange, London: Verso, 2001. Translation by Chris Turner of *L'Échange impossible*.

The Mirror of Production, St. Louis: Telos, 1975. Translation by Mark Poster of *Le Miroir de la production*.

Paroxysm: Interviews with Philippe Petit, London: Verso, 1998. Translation by Chris Turner of *Le Paroxyste indifférent*.

The Perfect Crime, London: Verso, 1996. Translation by Chris Turner of *Le Crime parfait*.

Photographies, 1985–1998, Graz, Neue Galerie and Ostfildern-Ruit: Hatje Cantz, 1999 (multilingual).

Screened Out, London: Verso, 2002. Translation by Chris Turner of *Écran total*.

Seduction, London: Macmillan, 1990. Translation by Brian Singer of *De la séduction*.

In the Shadow of the Silent Majorities, New York: Semiotext[e], 1983. Translation by Paul Foss, Paul Patton and John Johnston of *À l'Ombre des majorités silencieuses*.

Simulacra and Simulation, Ann Arbor, MI: University of Michigan Press, 1994. Translation by Sheila Faria Glaser of *Simulacres et simulation*.

The Singular Objects of Architecture, Minneapolis: University of Minnesota Press, 2002. Translation by Robert Bononno of *Les Objets singuliers*.

The Spirit of Terrorism, London: Verso, 2002. Translation by Chris Turner of *L'Esprit du terrorisme*.

Symbolic Exchange and Death, London: Sage, 1993. Translation by Iain Hamilton Grant of *L'Échange symbolique et la mort*.

The System of Objects, London: Verso, 1996. Translation by James Benedict of *Le Système des objets*.

The Transparency of Evil: Essays on Extreme Phenomena, London: Verso, 1993. Translation by James Benedict of *La Transparence du Mal*.

The Uncollected Baudrillard, London: Sage, 2001. Edited by Gary Genosko.

The Vital Illusion, New York: Columbia University Press, 2000.

'When Bataille attacked the metaphysical principle of economy', *Canadian Journal of Political and Social Theory*, 11(3) (1987), pp. 57–62. Translation by David James Miller of 'Quand Bataille . . .'.

'The Year 2000 Will Not Happen', in E.A. Grosz *et al.* (eds), *FuturFall: Excursions into Post-Modernity*, Sydney: Power Institute, pp. 18–28.

Baudrillard: in French

Le Système des objets, Paris: Gallimard, 1968.

La Société de la consommation, Paris: Gallimard, 1970.

Pour une critique de l'économie politique du signe, Paris: Gallimard, 1970.

Le Miroir de la production, Paris: Casterman, 1973.

L'Échange symbolique et la mort, Paris: Gallimard, 1976.

'Quand Bataille a attaqué le principe métaphysique de l'économie', *La Quinzaine littéraire*, 234 (June 1976), pp. 4–5.

Oublier Foucault, Paris: Galilée, 1977.

L'Ange de stuc, Paris: Galilée, 1978.

De la séduction, Paris: Denoël/Gonthier, 1979.

À l'Ombre des majorités silencieuses, Paris: Denoël/Gonthier, 1982.

Les Stratégies fatales, Paris: Grasset, 1983.

Please Follow Me (with Sophie Calle), Paris: Éditions de l'Étoile, 1983.

La Gauche divine, Paris: Grasset, 1985.

'L'an 2000 ne passera pas', *Traverses* 33–4 (1985), pp. 8–16.

Amérique, Paris: Grasset, 1986.

L'Autre par lui-même: habilitation, Paris: Galilée, 1987.

Cool Memories: 1980–1985, Paris: Galilée, 1987.

La Transparence du Mal: essai sur les phénomènes extrêmes, Paris: Galilée, 1990.

Cool Memories II: 1987–1990, Paris: Galilée, 1990.

Cool Memories I and II, Paris: Galilée, 1990.

La Guerre du Golfe n'a pas eu lieu, Paris: Galilée, 1991.

L'Illusion de la fin, ou la grève des événements, Paris: Galilée, 1992.

Figures de l'altérité (with Marc Guillaume), Paris: Éditions Descartes, 1992.

Le Crime parfait, Paris: Galilée, 1995.

Fragments: Cool Memories III, 1991–1995, Paris: Galilée, 1995.
Le Paroxyste indifférent: entretiens avec Philippe Petit, Paris: Grasset, 1997.
L'Échange impossible, Paris: Galilée, 1999.
Cool Memories IV: 1995–2000, Paris: Galilée, 2000.
Les Objets singuliers: architecture et philosophie (with Jean Nouvel), Paris: Calmann-Lévy, 2000.
Mots de passe, Paris: Pauvert, 2000.
Le Ludique et le policier, Paris: Sens & Tonka, 2001.
Télémorphose, Paris: Sens & Tonka, 2001.
D'un fragment l'autre: entretiens avec François L'Yonnet, Paris: Albin Michel, 2001.
L'Esprit du terrorisme, Paris: Galilée, 2002.
Power Inferno, Paris: Galilée, 2002.
'Le masque de la guerre', *Libération*, 10 March 2003, p. 8.
'Les suicidés du spectacle', *Libération*, 16 July 2003, p. 5.

Works by other writers

Agamben, Giorgio (1998) *Homo Sacer: Sovereign Power and Bare Life*, Stanford, CA: Stanford University Press.
Agamben, Giorgio (1999) *Remnants of Auschwitz: The Witness and the Archive*, New York: Zone.
Arendt, Hannah (1994) *Eichmann in Jerusalem: A Report on the Banality of Evil*, New York and London: Penguin.
Art of the Twentieth Century (1998) (2 vols), Cologne: Taschen.
Ballard, J.G. (1990) *War Fever*, London: Collins.
Ballard, J.G. (1995) *Crash*, London: Vintage.
Barthes, Roland (1974) *The Pleasure of the Text*, New York: Hill and Wang.
Barthes, Roland (1975) *S/Z*, New York: Hill and Wang.
Barthes, Roland (1977) 'Rhetoric of the Image', in *Image, Music, Text*, New York: Hill and Wang, pp. 32–51.
Barthes, Roland (1981) *Camera Lucida: Reflections on Photography*, London: Vintage.
Bataille, Georges (1985) *Visions of Excess: Selected Writings, 1927–1939*, ed. Allan Stoekl, Minneapolis: University Of Minnesota Press.
Bataille, Georges (1991a) *The Accursed Share*, New York: Zone.

Bataille, Georges (1991b) *The Accursed Share*, vols II and III: *The History of Eroticism and Sovereignty*, New York: Zone.

Baudelaire, Charles (1995) *The Painter of Modern Life and Other Essays*, London: Phaidon.

Benjamin, Walter (1992) *Illuminations*, London: Collins.

Best, Steven and Kellner, Douglas (1991) *Postmodern Theory: Critical Interrogations*, Basingstoke: Macmillan.

Bogard, William (1996) *The Simulation of Surveillance: Hypercontrol in Telematic Societies*, Cambridge: Cambridge University Press.

Bookchin, Murray (1977) *Post-Scarcity Anarchism*, Palo Alto, CA: Ramparts Press.

Borges, Jorge-Luis (1975) *A Universal History of Infamy*, London: Penguin.

Bottomore, Tom (ed.) (1991) *A Dictionary of Marxist Thought*, Oxford: Blackwell.

Butler, Rex (1999) *Jean Baudrillard: The Defence of the Real*, London: Sage.

Canetti, Elias (1973) *Crowds and Power*, London: Penguin.

Canetti, Elias (1985) *The Human Province*, London: Deutsch.

Carrier, David (2000) 'Baudrillard as Philosopher, or the End of Abstract Painting', in M. Gane (ed.), *Jean Baudrillard*, vol. IV London: Sage, pp. 20–36.

Chomsky, Noam (1989) *The Culture of Terrorism*, London: Pluto.

Chomsky, Noam (2001) *9/11*, New York: Seven Stories Press.

Cixous, Hélène (1979) 'Portrait of Dora', in *Benmussa Directs: Portraits of Dora and the Singular Life of Albert Nobbs*, London: John Calder, pp. 27–67.

Connor, Steven (1989) *Postmodernist Culture: An Introduction to Theories of the Contemporary*, Oxford: Blackwell.

Debord, Guy (1983) *Society of the Spectacle*, Detroit: Black and Red.

Deleuze, Gilles (1991) *Masochism*, New York: Zone.

Derrida, Jacques (1978) 'Cogito and the History of Madness', in *Writing and Difference*, London: Routledge, pp. 31–63.

Derrida, Jacques (1992) *Given Time I: Counterfeit Money*, Chicago: Chicago University Press.

Easton Ellis, Bret (1999) *Glamorama*, London: Picador.

Evans, Jessica and Hall, Stuart (eds), (1999) *Visual Culture: The Reader*, London: Sage.

Featherstone, Mike (1991) *Consumer Culture and Postmodernism*, London: Sage.

Foster, Hal (ed.) (1990) *Postmodern Culture*, London: Pluto.

Foucault, Michel (1970) *The Order of Things: An Archaeology of the Human Sciences*, London: Tavistock.

Foucault, Michel (1977) *Discipline and Punish*, London: Allen Lane.

Foucault, Michel (1979) *The History of Sexuality*, vol. I, Harmondsworth: Penguin.

Franko B (2003) *still life*, London: Black Dog.

Freud, Sigmund (1959) 'The Question of Lay Analysis', *Standard Edition* 20, London: Hogarth Press, pp. 183–258.

Freud, Sigmund (1986) *The Essentials of Psychoanalysis*, London: Penguin.

Gane, Mike (1991a) *Baudrillard's Bestiary: Baudrillard and Culture*, London: Routledge.

Gane, Mike (1991b) *Baudrillard: Critical and Fatal Theory*, London: Routledge.

Gane, Mike (2000a) *Jean Baudrillard: In Radical Uncertainty*, London: Pluto.

Gane, Mike (ed.) (2000b) *Jean Baudrillard* (4 vols), London: Sage.

Gane, Mike (2001) 'Reversible Feminism', *Semiotic Review of Books* 11 (3), pp. 2–4.

Genosko, Gary (1998) *Baudrillard and Signs: Signification Ablaze*, London: Routledge.

Genosko, Gary (1999) *McLuhan and Baudrillard: The Masters of Implosion*, London: Routledge.

Grace, Victoria (2000) *Baudrillard's Challenge: A Feminist Reading*, London: Routledge.

Grosz, E.A. *et al.* (eds) (1986) *FuturFall: Excursions into Post-Modernity*, Sydney: Power Institute.

Halley, Peter (1992) 'Nature and Culture', in C. Harrison and P. Wood (eds), *Art in Theory*, Oxford: Blackwell, pp. 1071–4.

Halley, Peter 'The Crisis in Geometry', largeglass.com.

Harrison, Charles and Wood, Paul (eds) (1992) *Art in Theory, 1900–1990: An Anthology of Changing Ideas*, Oxford: Blackwell.

Hegel, G.W.F. (1977) *The Phenomenology of Spirit*, Oxford: Oxford University Press.

Horrocks, Christopher (1999) *Baudrillard and the Millennium*, Cambridge: Icon.

Horrocks, Christopher and Jevtic, Zoran (1996) *Baudrillard for Beginners*, Cambridge: Icon.

Hughes, Robert (1997) *American Visions: The Epic History of Art in America*, London: Harvill Press.

Jencks, Charles (1991) *The Language of Postmodern Architecture*, London: Academy.

Kellner, Douglas (1989) *Jean Baudrillard: From Marxism to Postmodernism and Beyond*, Cambridge: Polity.

Kellner, Douglas (ed.) (1994) *Baudrillard: A Critical Reader*, Oxford: Blackwell.

Kroker, Arthur (1993) *Spasm: Virtual Reality, Android Music, Electric Flesh*, New York: St. Martins Press.

Kroker, Arthur and Cook, David (1988) *The Postmodern Scene: Excremental Culture and Hyper-Aesthetics*, London: Macmillan.

Kroker, Arthur and Kroker, Marilouise (1987) *Body Invaders: Panic Sex in America*, London: Macmillan.

Kroker, Arthur, Kroker, Marilouise and Cook, David (1989) *Panic Encyclopedia*, Montreal: New World Perspectives.

Lane, Richard J. (2000) *Jean Baudrillard*, London: Routledge.

Levin, Charles (1996) *Jean Baudrillard: A Study in Cultural Metaphysics*, London: Prentice Hall.

Lévi-Strauss, Claude (1952) *Race and History*, Paris: UNESCO.

Lyotard, Jean-François (1993) *Libidinal Economy*, London: Athlone.

McLuhan, Marshall (1964) *Understanding Media: The Extensions of Man*, London: Routledge.

McLuhan, Marshall and Fiore, Quentin (1967) *The Medium is the Massage*, Harmondsworth: Penguin.

McLuhan, Marshall and Fiore, Quentin (1968) *War and Peace in the Global Village*, New York: Bantam.

Marx, Karl (1976) *Capital*, vol. I, London: Penguin.

Mauss, Marcel (1967) *The Gift: Form and Function of Exchange in Archaic Societies*, New York: Norton.

Merrin, William (1994) 'Uncritical Criticism? Norris, Baudrillard and the Gulf War', *Economy and Society* 23 (4), pp. 433–58.

Nietzsche, Friedrich (1968) *The Will to Power*, New York: Vintage.

Nietzsche, Friedrich (1971) *The Twilight of the Idols*, Harmondsworth: Penguin.

Nietzsche, Friedrich (1989) *On the Genealogy of Morals/Ecce Homo*, New York: Vintage.

Norris, Christopher (1990) *What's Wrong with Postmodernism: Critical Theory and the Ends of Philosophy*, Hemel Hempstead: Harvester Wheatsheaf.

Norris, Christopher (1992) *Uncritical Theory: Postmodernism, Intellectuals and the Gulf War*, London: Lawrence and Wishart.

O'Brien, Flann (1988) *The Poor Mouth*, London: Flamingo.

Pefanis, Julian (1992) *Heterology and the Postmodern: Bataille, Baudrillard and Lyotard*, Durham, NC, and London: Duke University Press.

Plant, Sadie (1993) 'Baudrillard's Women: The Eve of Seduction', in C. Rojek and B.S. Turner (eds), *Forget Baudrillard?*, London: Routledge, pp. 88–106.

Ratcliff, Carter (2000) 'The Work of Roy Lichtenstein in the Age of Walter Benjamin's and Jean Baudrillard's Popularity', in M. Gane (ed.), *Jean Baudrillard*, vol. IV, London: Sage, pp. 49–66.

Reader, Keith A. (1987) *Intellectuals and the Left in France since 1968*, Basingstoke: Macmillan.

Rojek, Chris and Turner, Bryan S. (eds) (1993) *Forget Baudrillard?*, London: Routledge.

Ruddick, Nicholas (1992) 'Ballard/Crash/Baudrillard', *Science Fiction Studies*, 19, pp. 354–60.

Sahlins, Marshall (1974) *Stone Age Economics*, London: Tavistock.

Smith, M.W. (2001) *Reading Simulacra*, Albany, NY: SUNY Press.

Sokal, Alan and Bricmont, Jean (1998) *Intellectual Impostures*, London: Profile.

Stearns, William and Chaloupka, William (eds) (1992) *Jean Baudrillard*, Basingstoke: Macmillan.

Stiles, Kristine and Selz, Peter (eds) (1996) *Contemporary Art: A Sourcebook of Artists' Writings*, Berkeley: University of California Press.

symbiotica.uwa.edu.au

Virilio, Paul (1986) *Speed and Politics*, New York: Semiotext[e].

Virilio, Paul (1991) *The Aesthetics of Disappearance*, New York: Semiotext[e].

Virilio, Paul (2002) *Desert Screen*, New York: Continuum.

Wittig, Monique (1992) *The Straight Mind*, Boston: Beacon Press.
Yeghiayan, Eddie 'Jean Baudrillard: A Bibliography', sun3.lib.uci.edu/indiv/scctr/Wellek/baudrillard/index.html
Zurbrugg, Nicholas (1994) 'Baudrillard, Modernism, Postmodernism', in D. Kellner (ed.), *Baudrillard: A Critical Reader*, Oxford: Blackwell, pp. 229–55.
Zurbrugg, Nicholas (ed.) (1997) *Jean Baudrillard: Art and Artefact*, London: Sage.

Index